Decades of American History

AMERICA IN THE 1980s

MICHELE L. CAMARDELLA

Facts On File, Inc.

A Stonesong Press Book
Decades of American History: *America in the 1980s*

Facts On File, Inc.
132 West 31st Street
New York NY 10001

Library of Congress Cataloging-in-Publication Data

Camardella, Michele L.
  America in the 1980s / Michele L. Camardella.
    p. cm.—(Decades of American history)
  "A Stonesong Press book."
  Includes bibliographical references and index.
  ISBN 0-8160-5644-7
  1. United States—Politics and government—1981–1989—Juvenile literature.
  2. Reagan, Ronald—Juvenile literature. 3. Nineteen eighties—Juvenile
    literature. I. Title. II. Series.

  E876.C36 2005
  973.927—dc22   2005012438

Text design by Laura Smyth, Smythetype
Photo research by Larry Schwartz
Cover design by Pehrsson Design

Printed in the United States of America

VB PKG 10 9 8 7 6 5 4 3 2 1

This book is printed on acid-free paper.

CONTENTS

CHAPTER 1

A NEW DECADE IN AMERICA, 1980

THE 1980s WERE YEARS OF EXCESS AND of achievement, of economic turmoil for some, and economic advancement for others. In 1980, Jimmy Carter lost his bid for a second term, and Ronald Reagan became the nation's 40th president. Meanwhile, unemployment and inflation rates ebbed and then rose, creating a virtual roller coaster ride for the American people. The automotive industry, manufacturing, and family farming also suffered severe hits in the 1980s.

President Jimmy Carter waves from *Air Force One*. (*Jimmy Carter Library*)

Yuppies' leisure spending grew in the 1980s, as young people spent money on the latest designer sunglasses and fashionably distressed jeans and leather jackets. *(Levis)*

The word became smaller as the Soviet Union went from being viewed as an evil empire to being seen as an ally. The wall that separated East and West Berlin for almost three decades came down—and the walls that separated eastern Europe from democracy and the rest of the world dissolved as well.

The decade is often associated with greed, conspicuous consumption, and a return to traditional values and social mores. The rich got richer, the poor got poorer and the chasm between the haves and the have-nots grew ever larger. Young urban, upwardly mobile professionals, deemed yuppies, were the most obvious example of conspicuous consumption, driving luxury cars, taking exotic vacations, buying gourmet groceries, and investing in gym memberships in order to better fit into their designer-label clothes. Mergers, acquisitions and buy-outs allowed big companies to grow even bigger, and the major players in the business world to play even harder.

FROM PEANUT FARMER TO PRESIDENT

The 39th president, James Earl Carter Jr., was a native of Plains, Georgia. A graduate of the U.S. Naval Academy at Annapolis, Maryland, Carter had returned to Plains to run the family's peanut-farming business after his father's death in 1953. He served in politics on the state level throughout the early 1960s.

In the 1976 presidential election, Jimmy Carter and his running mate, Walter F. Mondale, defeated incumbent Republican President Gerald R. Ford and Vice President Nelson A. Rockefeller. When he took office, Carter had ambitious plans, but Congress, still stinging from the Watergate scandal, was uncooperative. Although Carter excelled at foreign relations, the U.S. economy took a beating in the late 1970s.

STAGFLATION

From the onset of his presidency, Carter had been plagued by economic woes, many of them stemming from the 1977 energy crisis that resulted from America's dependence on foreign oil. In April 1980, the unemployment rate hit 7 percent, and there were 7.3 million unemployed Americans. Inflation and interest rates rose, with interest rates hitting 18.5 percent that spring. Some predicted rates would top 20 percent in the near future, and inflation would rise 12 percent. Simultaneously, housing starts—the number of new homes upon which construction has begun—decreased by 6 percent, and the building industry experienced slowdowns and lay-offs. Automobile sales also suffered, down 24 percent from the previous year. This combination of high unemployment, high prices, and a slowed, stagnant economy came to be known as stagflation.

In May 1980, things got a little better as inflation dipped and interest rates decreased. Unemployment, however, remained a sore spot, hitting 7.8 percent that month, and housing starts and automobile sales failed to go up. In the second quarter of the year, corporate profits experienced their largest decrease to that point since World War II, dipping more than 18 percent.

BILLYGATE

In July 1980, it was disclosed that President Carter's brother, Billy, was under investigation by the Senate and the Justice Department because he had accepted $220,000 as part of a loan from Libya. Because he had failed to register as a foreign agent, his acceptance of the loan may have violated federal law. Billy had Libyan oil interests and had attended meetings with Libyan advisors meant to assist in the release of the U.S. hostages. Later Billy registered as a foreign agent and declared that he had received $220,000. However, his actions created questions. Was the White House involved? Why did it take Billy so long to come clean? Ultimately, the president was not accused of any wrongdoing, although many did question his judgment in using his good 'ol boy brother as a diplomat.

Congress bailed Chrysler out of bankruptcy by approving $1.5 billion in loans. By July 1980, there were 8.2 million unemployed Americans.

For most of 1980, Carter's proposed initiatives, including a youth employment program for minority teenagers and a proposal for improved health benefits for underprivileged children, fell by the wayside. Congress also rejected Carter's proposal for an Energy Mobilization Board, and his plans to impose a surcharge of 10 cents per gallon on imported oil. Congress, did, however, pass the Energy Security Act, which focused on the development of alternative energy sources. Carter was also successful in the passage of a $1.6 billion superfund earmarked for toxic waste. On November 12, Congress approved the Alaska National Interest Lands Conservation Act (ANILCA), sweeping legislation that protected over 100 million acres of Alaskan land. The act effectively tripled the amount of U.S. land deemed wilderness and doubled the size of the national parks and wildlife refuge system. As a result of ANILCA, 10 new national parks were created, and the acreage of three established parks increased.

Former Minnesota senator Walter Mondale (left), pictured here with President Jimmy Carter, served as vice president during the Carter administration. *(Jimmy Carter Library)*

The Alaskan National Interest Lands Conservation Act (ANILCA) protected more than 100 million acres of land in Alaska such as Glacier Bay National Preserve, shown here. *(National Park Service)*

ABSCAM

In February, it was disclosed that FBI agents posing as wealthy Arabs had successfully coerced government officials and members of Congress into taking bribes from a fictitious sheik in exchange for political favors. Codenamed Abscam, the operation resulted in indictments against seven members of Congress and 12 other individuals. In August 1980, Representative Michael Myers, a Democrat from Pennsylvania, and three others were found guilty of taking bribes. Myers was the first Congressman to be expelled from the House on corruption charges. Representatives John Jenrette of South Carolina, John M. Murphy of New York, and Frank Thompson Jr. of New Jersey, were also found guilty at later trials.

THE HOSTAGE CRISIS

Iranian militants stormed into the U.S. Embassy in Teheran on November 4, 1979, when they heard that the deposed shah of Iran, Mohammad Reza Shah Pahlavi, had arrived in the United States for treatment of cancer. The militants took the embassy staff hostage in the name of the cleric Ayatollah Ruhollah Khomeini, the anti-American leader of Iran's revolutionary government. Although the prime minister of Iran, Mehdi Bazargan, ordered the 60 hostages released, Khomeini refused to back him, using the opportunity to rid himself of the more moderate Bazargan, who resigned his office.

Iranian students studying in the United States immediately protested the shah's medical treatment and demanded that he be sent back to Iran. Their actions only increased anti-Iran sentiment in the United States. Congress introduced legislation to expel Iranian students, or at the least, to prohibit their protests. Iranian protesters were beaten in Beverly Hills, and American workers refused their services to Iranian ships and airliners.

A week after the takeover, Carter froze all Iranian assets in the United States and ceased the purchase of oil from Iran. He then proceeded to seek the release of the hostages through diplomatic means.

The hostage crisis was detailed nightly on the news. Americans tied yellow ribbons around trees in honor of the hostages. Unable to secure the hostages release through diplomatic means, Carter decided to go forward with a military plan, despite Secretary of State Cyrus Vance's requests to continue seeking a diplomatic resolution. On April 7, 1980, Carter announced his intentions to break diplomatic relations with Iran to the National Security Council In addition, he planned an embargo on all American goods to Iran, with the exception of medicine and food.

On April 25, 1980, the military operation planned to rescue the hostages failed, resulting in the deaths of eight American servicemen. The rescue plan involved eight military helicopters departing from the USS *Nimitz,* situated in the Gulf of Oman, traveling south of Teheran and then meeting with 90 rescue team members and their supplies. The plan included a helicopter rescue of the team and the hostages, and ultimately, plane transport to Saudi Arabia.

But problems cropped up as soon as the plan was activated. One helicopter suffered mechanical difficulties, while another got lost in a sandstorm and returned to the aircraft carrier. With two spare helicopters unavailable, the maneuver was already shaky. The mission was aborted when a third helicopter developed mechanical problems. As the rescue team boarded the transport planes to depart, one of the helicopters rose, banked, and cut into the fuselage of one of the planes, killing eight servicemen and burning four others. The remaining U.S. forces abandoned the other helicopters and the bodies of those who perished. The failure of the rescue plan and the deaths of American servicemen badly affected Carter's popularity.

In September 1980, Iran relayed through Germany's ambassador that they were willing to resume discussions regarding the hostage crisis. A delegation consisting of

An attempt to rescue American hostages being held in Iran resulted in the deaths of eight American servicemen when this helicopter crashed. *(AP/Wide World Photos)*

five representatives, including Deputy Secretary of State Warren Christopher, traveled to Bonn, West Germany, and met with a distant relative of Khomeini's, who relayed their discussion to the ayatollah. Unfortunately, the Iran-Iraq War—which would last eight years—began shortly thereafter, thereby delaying additional talks. Tensions between the two countries escalated into war when Iraq dismissed an agreement with Iran regarding the Shatt al-Arab waterway. (The Shatt al-Arab waterway was a bone of contention between Iran and Iraq, and it remains a source of conflict, as limited water access and unresolved maritime boundaries in the region persist.) Iraqi jets attacked 10 Iranian airfields later that month.

Comments made by the Iranian prime minister, as well as information that the hostages had all been regrouped at the embassy, seemed to imply that the Iranians were ready to release the hostages. A preelection release would surely cement Carter's win in November for a second term as president. But Carter's announcement on November 2 that the Iranians would release the hostages only if the conditions set forth by Khomeini were actually met hurt him in the election. While an October surprise—an event that occurs immediately prior to Election Day and impacts the vote—would have helped his chances, this last minute revelation seemed contrived and angered many voters.

Carter lost the presidential election to Ronald Reagan, yet he and a team of experts continued to work diligently to obtain the release of the hostages. Particularly difficult was Khomeini's demand that the assets of the former, and now deceased, shah be returned to Iran. Ultimately, a deal was reached when the United States promised $9 billion to Iran once the hostages were released. Although Carter and his team worked around the clock, the final negotiations were not competed until January 20, 1981—the day of Reagan's inauguration. There has been some speculation that Reagan's team interfered with the negotiations in order to ensure that the hostage release would not happen within Carter's last days, but these allegations have never been proven.

OTHER FOREIGN AFFAIRS

In December 1979, the Soviet Union (USSR) sent 85,000 troops to Afghanistan because it had begun to assert its independence from Soviet influence. In response to this Soviet aggression, on January 3, 1980, Carter requested that the Senate indefinitely postpone considering the SALT II agreement. The result of seven years of negotiation between the United States and the Soviet Union, this treaty called for limiting the weapons systems of each country.

The following day in a public address, the president announced an embargo on grain sales to the USSR and that the Soviets would not be allowed access to high technology equipment. In addition, he indicated a possible boycott of the 1980 Summer Olympics in Moscow. In a State of the Union address on January 23, the president made it abundantly clear that outside attempts to take over the Persian Gulf region were against the best interest of the United States and would be considered a confrontation and an invitation for the use of military force. This stance became know as the Carter Doctrine.

In addition, the president requested a 5 percent increase in military spending, as well as $400 million to aid Afghanistan's neighbor Pakistan. The Carter administration intended to increase the American military presence in the Persian Gulf. He also wanted all American males aged between 18 and 26 to register for a possible future draft.

Beginning in April 1980, boats brought approximately 125,000 Cuban refugees to the United States. Over the course of five months, approximately 80,000 refugees settled in metro Miami, Florida. These refugees joined an already large Cuban population in Dade County.

"While this invasion continues, we and the other nations of the world cannot conduct business as usual with the Soviet Union. . . . neither the American people nor I will support sending an Olympic team to Moscow."

—President Jimmy Carter, State of the Union address, January 23, 1980

RACIAL VIOLENCE

In May 1980, four white policemen charged with beating Arthur McDuffie, a black insurance salesman, to death were acquitted by an all-white jury in Tampa, Florida. Following the verdict, 16 people died in three days of violence that included looting, arson, and the destruction of cars in the Liberty section of Miami. Property damage totaled an estimated $100 million; 1,250 people were arrested and 300 were injured. Similarly, a riot ensued in Chattanooga, Tennessee, when an all-white jury found whites accused of killing blacks innocent. Other incidents occurred in Wichita, Kansas, and Boston, Massachusetts. The failing economy lent itself to discontent, as urban areas and minorities were hit hard by unemployment rates and higher priced goods.

1980 PRESIDENTIAL CAMPAIGN

Initially, Carter's handling of the hostage crisis helped redeem his image and was responsible for a surge in his popularity. A Gallup survey—named after statistician George H. Gallup, who devised a system of assessment of public opinion by questioning a representative sample—showed that Carter's public approval rating had increased from 30 percent to 61 percent since the start of the crisis. At one point, Carter had even trailed Senator Edward Kennedy in polls for the Democratic nomination. But as 1979 drew to a close, Carter regained his edge in the polls.

In the Democratic Party primaries known as Super Tuesday in June 1980, five of the eight states voted for Kennedy, although Carter retained the lead in terms of delegate votes. Even at the 1980 Democratic Convention, held in New York City, Kennedy did not completely give up. Although he subsequently withdrew his candidacy, Kennedy first ensured that some of his policies were included in the party platform.

Senator Edward Kennedy (left) vied for the Democratic nomination in 1980 against Jimmy Carter, while John Anderson (right) ran in the presidential election as an Independent candidate. *(Jimmy Carter Library)*

FROM ILLINOIS TO HOLLYWOOD TO THE PRESIDENCY

Ronald Wilson Reagan could not have picked a better time than 1980 to run for president of the United States of America. The former actor, who served as governor of California from 1967 through 1974, was the complete opposite of Jimmy Carter, the gentleman farmer from Georgia who was never quite able to win over Congress or the American public. Reagan's charisma and his congenial attitude proved too much for Democratic incumbent Carter.

Reagan, a graduate of Eureka College and an Illinois native, started his career as an actor. An initial screen test with Warner Brothers was a success, and Reagan appeared in over 50 films during the course of the next 27 years. From 1947 to 1952, Reagan served as the president of the Screen Actors Guild. During this time, he testified before the House Un-American Activities Committee, participating in the blacklisting of directors, writers, and actors accused of being communist sympathizers.

As his movie career waned in the mid-1950s, Reagan became the host of television's *General Electric Theater*. In fact, as the host and a spokesman for the company, Reagan made speeches focusing on the perils of government intervention at GE plants nationwide. Eventually, the company deemed his comments too controversial and fired him in 1962.

Reagan campaigned for Richard Nixon in the 1962 California gubernatorial election, and for Barry Goldwater in the 1964 presidential election. During the last week of the campaign, Reagan made a nationally televised speech about his conversion from Democrat to Republican. Although Reagan had been a Democrat and a fan of Franklin Delano Roosevelt as a young man, his experiences in Hollywood and with General Electric had led him to embrace Republican ideals. The speech raised $1 million in contributions to the Republican Party and effectively launched Reagan's

Prior to his political career, Ronald Reagan gained fame as an actor in films such as *Knute Rockne: All-American* (1940). *(Ronald Reagan Library)*

Governor and Mrs. Reagan are pictured with their children, Ron Jr. and Patti, in this 1967 photo. *(Ronald Reagan Library)*

political career. It also convinced many prominent Republicans that he was the ideal candidate for the 1966 California gubernatorial election.

To counter incumbent Democratic governor Edmund "Pat" Brown's assertions that an actor was unqualified to be governor, Reagan campaigned as an everyday citizen who wanted to undo the mess that politicians had made of California. Brown lost the election by 1 million votes, the largest margin in history at that time. Assuming office in 1967, Reagan reformed California's welfare programs and instituted a major tax increase to counter the large deficit left by his predecessor. He served as governor for two terms, leaving office in 1974. Reagan's plans to run for president in 1976 were dashed by Nixon's resignation in 1974 after the Watergate scandal, and Vice President Gerald Ford's assumption of the office. Reagan lost the 1976 Republican nomination to Ford by 60 votes.

In 1980, making another run for the presidency, Republican candidate Reagan and his running mate,

George H. W. Bush, promised to increase defense spending, cut taxes, limit the growth of the federal government, and ban abortion. This appealed to conservative Americans. They blamed the tolerance of a liberal government for increased crime rates, divorce, welfare, promiscuity, and drug abuse.

Reagan referred to the sum of the unemployment and inflation rates, which totaled more than 20, as the misery index, and asked Americans, "Are you better off today than you were four years ago?" Apparently, the answer was a resounding "No." Carter's inability to win Congress' support, coupled with a problematic economy, conservative discontent and foreign policy debacles such as the hostage crisis in Iran resulted in a significant victory for the Republican Party in the 1980 elections. Reagan won 51 percent of the popular vote (43,195,000) and 483 votes in the Electoral College, while Carter received 41 percent of the popular vote (34,911,000) and just 49 Electoral College votes. Independent candidate John Anderson finished with 6.6 percent of the popular vote (5,581,000), enough to make him a spoiler in the key states of New York and Florida, but not enough to make him the reason for Carter's loss. Interestingly, voter turnout was lower than it had been since 1948. In addition to Reagan's presidential victory, the Republicans gained seats in the House of Representatives and enjoyed their first Senate majority since 1952.

The Republican party rallied behind Ronald Reagan at the 1980 convention. *(Ronald Reagan Library)*

TELEVISION

By 1980, 23 percent of the American households received basic cable, up from 8 percent 10 years earlier. Pay channels such as Home Box Office (HBO) and

In March 1980, the unemployment rate in Detroit, Michigan, was 24 percent.

"To provide information to people when it wasn't available before... to offer those who want it a choice;... I dedicate the News Channel of America—the Cable News Network."

—Ted Turner, during the June 1, 1980, dedication of the Cable News Network (CNN) from its Atlanta headquarters

On April 29, 1980, an estimated quarter to half million people attended the Washington for Jesus rally, a marathon prayer meeting.

Showtime could be found in 12 percent of the American homes in 1980. Not quite a threat to the big three networks yet, cable television was planting the seeds for future expansion.

Launched on June 1, 1980, Ted Turner's Cable News Network (CNN) was committed completely to covering the news. The innovative network made it possible to get headlines and breaking news from around the globe 24 hours a day. As a response to CNN, network news took on more of a news magazine format. This experimentation with formats also led to an increased emphasis on entertainment reporting.

On network television, the prime time soap opera *Dallas* had viewers enthralled. On March 21, 1980, the character they loved to hate, J. R. Ewing, was shot. All summer, Americans wondered, "Who shot J. R.?" A strike by the American Federation of Television and Radio Artists, meanwhile, delayed television production from July 22 to October 3 and the start of the fall television season, forcing viewers to endure a long wait until the season premiere on November 7. Season-end cliffhanger episodes soon became a staple of television dramas.

On other television networks, *Little House on the Prairie* fans watched as Almanzo proposed to Laura Ingalls, and Nellie Olson found someone to marry. The 12-hour, $22 million miniseries *Shogun,* based on James Clavell's best-selling novel, aired for five nights in September.

FILM

In 1980, two sequels—*The Empire Strikes Back* and *Superman II*—scored big at the box office. *Airplane!* spoofed the disaster films that were so common in the 1970s. Jack Nicholson terrified Shelley Duvall—and viewers—in *The Shining*. Robert Redford made a stunning directorial debut with *Ordinary People,* starring

Donald Sutherland, Mary Tyler Moore, and newcomer Timothy Hutton as a family dealing with a devastating loss. The film won the Oscar for Best Picture, Redford received the award for Best Director, and Hutton walked away with the statuette for Best Supporting Actor. Robert DeNiro won the Best Actor Oscar for *Raging Bull,* and Sissy Spacek received the Best Actress award for her mesmerizing turn as Loretta Lynn in the biographical *Coal Miner's Daughter.*

MUSIC

Newcomer Christopher Cross swept the Grammy awards with his self-titled debut album, winning Album of the Year, the hit single "Sailing" taking both Record of the Year and Song of the Year, and Cross being named Best New Artist. The remnants of disco still lingered in the hit "Please Don't Go" by K. C. and The Sunshine Band. The punk-influenced Blondie scored big with "Call Me," and the title single from the film *Fame* had kids everywhere wishing they could dance on a yellow cab in the middle of a New York City street. There was also a resurgence in country music, which accounted for 14.3 percent of all record sales in the United States. By 1980, there were 1,534 full-time country music stations as opposed to only 81 just 19 years earlier.

On a somber note, millions of fans around the world mourned the death of John Lennon on December 8. The former Beatle was shot by Mark David Chapman outside the Dakota, the New York City apartment building in which Lennon lived. Lennon was just 40 when he was killed. Almost a week later, more than 10 million fans observed 10 minutes of silence in his memory.

Millions of fans worldwide mourned the death of former Beatle John Lennon, who was shot and killed by Mark David Chapman upon returning home from a recording studio. *(AP/Wide World Photos)*

"Do you believe in miracles? Yes!"

—ABC announcer Al Michaels

SPORTS

Undoubtedly, the major sport story of 1980 was the U.S. hockey team's win, dubbed the Miracle on Ice, at the Winter Olympics in Lake Placid, New York. Coach Herb Brooks focused on discipline and speed, grooming the team as they played exhibition games throughout Europe and North America. At the Olympics, the U.S. team scored a last-minute goal in its first game against Sweden, ending in a 2-2 tie. They won the next game against Czechoslovakia 3-2, and then enjoyed two more decisive victories over Norway (5-1) and Romania (7-2). In their fifth game, the U.S. team eliminated West Germany, with a score of 4-2.

Game six, played on February 20, 1980, pitted the United States against the Soviet Union, who had completely dominated the sport in the late 1970s. A dramatic game ensued, where the U.S. team relied on its secret weapon: speed. With a score of USA 4 and USSR 3 in the third period, the U.S. team held the Soviets at bay for 10 more minutes of play. Despite the win over the USSR, the U.S. team had to defeat Finland for the gold medal. If they lost and the USSR defeated Sweden, the Soviets would go home with the gold. The U.S. hock-

The U.S. hockey team won the gold medal at the 1980 Olympics, defeating the Soviet Union in a thrilling semifinal and then beating Finland in the finals. *(AP/Wide World Photos)*

ey team prevailed and came back from trailing Finland at the end of the second period to win with a final score of USA 4 and Finland 2.

Exactly two months after the winter games, the United States threatened to boycott the Moscow Summer Olympics in protest against the Soviet invasion of Afghanistan in 1979. Ultimately, the United States carried out its threat and did not attend the Moscow games. The games, the first to be held in a communist nation, were boycotted by 62 other nations. The National Broadcasting Company (NBC) opted not to broadcast the games, losing approximately $22 million as a result.

In other sports news, tennis champion Bjørn Bjorg set a record by winning the men's title at Wimbledon for the fifth consecutive year. He lost the U.S. Open, however, to John McEnroe, who claimed that title for the second year in a row. That same year, Chris Evert Lloyd won the woman's title at the U.S. Open for the fifth time in six years.

In August, New York Yankee Reggie Jackson hit home run number 400 in his career. Later that year, outfielder Dave Winfield signed a contract with the Yankees for a reported $22 million over 10 years, making him the highest paid player of team sports in U.S. history. Meanwhile, the 1980 World Series be tween Philadelphia and Kansas City was the highest rated in history, viewed in 40 percent of all U.S. homes that had televisions.

> **T**he best-selling *The Official Preppy Handbook* elevated the term *preppy* to new status. This satirical look at the lifestyle of the wealthy poked fun at the nicknames, traditions, fashion, and pastimes of the upper crust.

Mount Saint Helens, located south of Seattle, erupted on May 18, 1980, killing 57 people, thousands of animals, and millions of salmon, and wreaking havoc on the local terrain. *(J. Franklin, USDA Forest Service)*

SCIENCE AND TECHNOLOGY

On May 18, 1980, the volcano Mount St. Helens erupted following an earthquake below the mountain that measured 5.1 on the Richter scale. (The magnitude of

Acid rain, caused by pollution, became a global concern throughout the 1980s. This lake in the Rockies is ringed by trees killed by acid rain.
(F. Valenzuela, USDA Forest Service)

Arthur Fry, a chemist at 3M, invented Post-It notes in 1980.
(3M)

an earthquake is measured on a Richter scale, which was originally developed by Charles Richter and Beno Gutenberg to make more quantitative measures of the relative sizes of earthquakes in southern California.) Located in the Cascade Range in southwestern Washington State, the volcano had been dormant for more than 120 years. The blast resulted in a huge landslide and a lateral blast of materials that hit 300 miles per hour, and within 15 minutes a column of gas and ash extended more than 15 miles into the sky. It resulted in the death of 57 people and damage to approximately 200 homes and 27 bridges. In addition, according to the U.S. Geological Survey, some 7,000 big game animals and millions of salmon in hatcheries were killed, and trees totaling 4 billion board feet of timber—or enough to build 300,000 two-bedroom homes—were blown down.

In 1980, an International Joint Committee was established between the United States and Canada to investigate air quality and the acid rain issue. A growing problem since the 1950s, acid rain was caused by pollutants from fossil fuel emissions, such as those from automobiles and factories, which react in the atmosphere to cause acid rain, which contains high levels of sulfuric and nitric acid. Acid rain was found to contaminate drinking water and have negative effects on vegetation, wildlife, and aquatic life. It also damaged human-made buildings and marble structures such as statues.

CHAPTER 2

AN ACTOR TAKES ON WASHINGTON, D.C., 1981–1982

President and Mrs. Reagan attended eight inaugural balls during the evening of January 20, 1981, including one at the Air and Space Museum. *(Ronald Reagan Library)*

O N JANUARY 20, 1981, JUST TWO weeks prior to his 70th birthday, Ronald Reagan was sworn in as the 40th president of the United States of America. He was the oldest man in the history of the United States to assume the office. The new president began his first term on a high note. Soon after the inaugural ceremony, he announced that Iran had agreed to release the U.S. Embassy employees who had been held hostage for 444 days. This accomplishment instilled confidence in the new administration, particularly since the Carter administration's efforts to

First Lady Rosalynn Carter shopped off the rack, unlike First Lady Nancy Reagan, who was criticized for her expensive, designer taste. *(Jimmy Carter Library)*

rescue the hostages had continuously failed. Ironically, Carter had spent his last days in the White House successfully negotiating the release of the 52 hostages. In the end, $8 billion in Iranian assets that had been frozen in American banks were released as part of the deal.

At the time, Reagan's was the most expensive inauguration in history, costing $8 million. Paying homage to Reagan's western roots, the inauguration ceremony was held at the West Front of the Capitol, an inauguration first. After the swearing-in and the conclusion of his speech, Reagan completed his first action as president and suspended government hiring, fulfilling a campaign promise. Next, a luncheon was held at the Capitol, followed by a parade attended by over 300,000 people and featuring 8,000 marchers, 450 equestrian teams, and representatives from various American cultural and regional groups.

Later that evening, President and Mrs. Reagan attended each of the eight inaugural balls. The new first lady's designer inaugural attire was said to have cost $25,000—a stark contrast to practical former First Lady Rosalynn Carter's off the rack wardrobe. In retrospect, the inauguration was an indicator of the excess that would follow throughout the decade.

NANCY REAGAN

Nancy Reagan's extravagant, glamorous style was completely opposite that of former First Lady Rosalynn Carter. Her designer clothes and star-studded White House parties were not well received given the struggling economy. Mrs. Reagan raised $800,000 in private donations to refurbish the White House but received negative press for spending $200,000 on new china. To counter the criticism, the first lady shifted the focus of her charity work and embraced the anti-drug cause, beginning the "Just Say No" campaign. Mrs. Reagan was accused of having too much influence over her husband's decisions, particularly during his second term. Former chief of staff Donald Regan also claimed that the first lady insisted that her astrologer's predictions regarding the president be taken seriously.

Nancy Reagan poked fun at her high-maintenance image by dressing in secondhand clothes for an event at the Gridiron Club. (*Ronald Reagan Library*)

"In this present crisis, government is not the solution to our problem. Government is the problem."

—Ronald Reagan, Inaugural address, 1981

REAGANOMICS

The Reagan administration's primary focus was invigorating the lagging American economy. His economic plan, deemed Reaganomics, was based on supply-side economics. It contended that by implementing tax cuts, wealthy Americans and corporations would spend

Budget director David Stockman admitted in an interview that the president's economic plan did not add up. *(Jimmy Carter Library)*

"None of us really understands what's going on with all these numbers."

—David Stockman, director of the Office of Management and Budget, quoted in *Atlantic Monthly,* December 1981

more money overall, thereby supporting the economy and helping pay down the federal deficit, the amount of money the government had to borrow every year to pay its bills. Simultaneously, the less affluent would benefit from the availability of cheaper goods and from a surge in jobs needed to meet the new demand for goods—a trickle down effect. The plan included major cuts in government spending as well—although Social Security and Medicare would be spared—and aspired to provide a balanced budget within the next three and a half years. The director of the Office of Management and Budget, David Stockman, admitted in a December 1981 interview in *Atlantic Monthly* that the plan was likely to cause the deficit to increase.

An advocate of a smaller government, Reagan eliminated 37,000 federal jobs in March 1981. After just one month in office, Reagan proposed $41.4 billion in budget cuts, and $53.9 billion in tax cuts intended to benefit workers and businesses. The Omnibus Budget Reconciliation Act of 1981 reduced the budgets of 212 federal programs, most of which aided the working poor, including food stamps, student loans, mass transit, and child nutrition programs. The Economic Recovery Tax Act of 1981, meanwhile, included reductions to personal income and business taxes (25 percent reductions over the course of three years), as well as to capital gains, inheritance, and gift taxes. Both programs were passed by Congress in July 1981, and signed by President Reagan on August 13, 1981.

Reagan's plan failed to spark the economy immediately. Although inflation dipped during his first year in office, interest rates rose to new heights. Banks increased their prime rates from 17 percent to 20.5 percent during the summer of 1981, and short-term interest rates increased to 18 percent from 13 percent. The stock and bond markets declined in August and September 1981, rather than rebounding as Reagan and his advisers had expected. In August 1981, the

President Reagan's plan to beef up U.S. defenses included the production of the B-1 bomber. *(DOD Defense Visual Information Center)*

United States entered a recession that would continue throughout the year and worsen in 1982.

While Reagan endorsed budget and tax cuts, he simultaneously embarked upon an expanded military program. He supported a gradual buildup of the military, the development of the Stealth bomber, the restoration of the B-1 bomber program, the deployment of the Missile Experimental (M-X) missile, and a navy numbering 600 ships. His initial five-year Defense Guidance Plan, introduced in 1982, included $1.6 trillion for defense spending.

"HONEY, I FORGOT TO DUCK"

On March 31, 1981, merely nine weeks after Reagan's inauguration, John W. Hinckley Jr., a drifter, made an attempt on the president's life. As Reagan left the Washington Hilton Hotel, Hinckley fired a .22 caliber revolver six times, striking Reagan, press secretary James Brady, Secret Service agent Timothy J. McCarthy, and District of Columbia police officer Thomas K. Delahanty. It was later learned that Hinckley was obsessed with actress Jodie Foster and was attempting

President Reagan survived an assassination attempt outside the Washington Hilton Hotel on March 31, 1981, just nine weeks after assuming office. *(Ronald Reagan Library)*

to impress her by imitating Travis Bickle, Robert DeNiro's character in the Martin Scorsese film *Taxi Driver*, in which Foster had starred. Hinckley, who was arrested at the scene, was found not guilty by reason of insanity at his trial on June 21, 1982, and was admitted to a hospital for the mentally ill.

Despite the fact that a bullet had punctured and collapsed one lung and still remained in his chest, Reagan continued to joke throughout the ordeal. "Honey, I forgot to duck," he famously quipped to his wife in the hospital.

That sentence further endeared him to the American people. The president appeared to bounce back quickly, signing legislation the next morning and making public appearances shortly after the shooting. In reality, however, his recovery took quite a few months. Amazingly, the three other victims survived

Hinckley's shots as well, although Brady was paralyzed for life, prompting both Brady and his wife, Sarah, to become major advocates for handgun control.

The assassination attempt also prompted some controversy within the White House. With press secretary James Brady wounded, his assistant, Larry Speakes, addressed the media but had little or no information to share regarding a succession plan should the president need surgery and require anesthesia. Speakes' unsettling performance before the media prompted Secretary of State Alexander Haig to take action. Soon, he was standing before the media trying to reassure the American public by stating that he was in control of the White House in the absence of the president and until the arrival of the vice president, who was in Texas. Unfortunately, Haig appeared nervous, and, in fact, gave the public the wrong information. Haig received much criticism for his assumption of power, as the Speaker of the House was officially third in the succession plan, followed by the president pro tempore of the Senate.

President Reagan is pictured addressing Congress for the first time following the attempt on his life as Vice President George Bush and Speaker of the House Tip O'Neill look on. *(Ronald Reagan Library)*

UNFRIENDLY SKIES

The skies were not friendly in August 1981, when 13,000 members of the Professional Air Traffic Controllers Organization (PATCO) went on strike seeking improved work conditions and better pay. Because PATCO members were federal employees, it was illegal for them to strike, and Reagan ordered them to return to work within 48 hours or lose their jobs. Flights were cancelled, delayed, and grounded as new hires underwent training to replace the striking members were fired on August 5. The action destroyed PATCO, which went bankrupt. Reagan's firm stance against strike, combined with his resiliency during and after the March 1981 assassination attempt, helped establish him as a force to be reckoned with early in his presidency.

"I hope you're all Republicans."

—Ronald Reagan, to doctors at George Washington University Hospital following an assassination attempt

REAGAN AND THE RELIGIOUS RIGHT

On September 25, 1981, Sandra Day O'Connor made history when she was sworn in as an associate justice on the Supreme Court, filling the seat left by the retirement of Potter Stewart. O'Connor was not only Reagan's first appointee to the court but also the first woman ever to be appointed to the court. Reagan's choice was a great disappointment to the religious right, a group that had supported him wholeheartedly during his campaign, largely because he claimed to be a proponent of traditional moral and family values. Not only was O'Connor a moderate conservative, but she was also pro-choice, had supported the Equal Rights Amendment (ERA), and did not have any religious affiliation.

The religious right, led largely by televangelist and founder of the Moral Majority Jerry Falwell, had worked hard to register voters and raise funds for Reagan's cause. Evangelical Christians had gained some political footing with the election of Jimmy Carter, an evangelical Christian himself, in 1976. As president, however, Carter had failed to champion many of the causes traditionally associated with the religious right. The group put their support behind Reagan presuming

Sandra Day O'Connor, pictured with Chief Justice Warren Burger and her husband John O'Connor, made history when she was sworn as the first female Supreme Court Justice. She retired from the court in 2005. *(Ronald Reagan Library)*

that he would support their agenda.

Christian conservatives were counting on Reagan to support their opposition to homosexual rights, pornography, abortion, and the passage of the ERA, among other issues. Initially, Reagan was accommodating. The first citizen's group welcomed to the Reagan White House—just two days after his inauguration—represented the right-to-life movement. This symbolic gesture, as well as an address by the secretary of Health and Human Services, Richard Schweiker, to 60,000 attendees of the annual March for Life, gave hope to anti-abortion groups. Soon, North Carolina senator Jesse Helms and Illinois congressman Henry Hyde cosponsored the Human Life Statute, a piece of legislation declaring that life began at conception. The statute would have allowed states to declare abortion murder. The bill did not pass in Congress, and Reagan did not throw any of his weight behind it. That was the first warning signal to the religious right that they might not have the White House support they expected.

Justice O'Connor's appointment was the second cause for concern. Then, Reagan failed to endorse the Family Protection Act, a 31-provision piece of legislation that had been developed by a coalition of political and religious conservatives. Among other things, the act called for the prohibition of abortion, supported the restoration of school prayer, gave parents and community groups the right to censor reading materials used in public schools, called for a tax break for wives and mothers who did not work outside of the home and tuition tax credits for children attend-

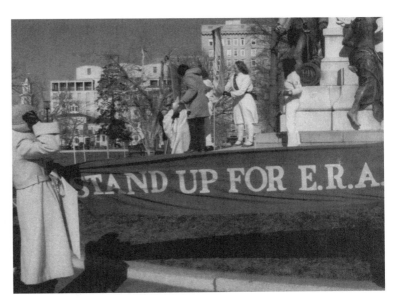

The Equal Rights Amendment remained a controversial topic throughout the 1980s, provoking both support and dissent. These supporters marched in 1980. *(Jimmy Carter Library)*

ing private school, promoted single-sex only sports activities at school, and banned a teenager's access to contraception unless a parent was notified. Rather than championing the causes of Christian conservatives, Reagan appeared to be dismissing their agenda.

Perhaps the greatest victories of the religious right in the early 1980s were the defeat of the ERA in 1982 and Reagan's support of a Constitutional amendment allowing prayer in school. The ERA, which called for an amendment to the Constitution declaring equal rights for both sexes under the law, had first been submitted to state legislatures for ratification in 1972. Despite an extension of three years to the seven-year ratification deadline, only 35 of the required 38 states had ratified the amendment. Because many conservative Christian groups supported the traditional family model, they were not fans of this progressive legislation and considered its defeat their victory.

In May 1982, Reagan held a press briefing to announce that he was supporting a prayer-in-school amendment. While the proposed amendment allowed for public prayer in school, it also did not mandate it. It would be two years until the Senate would vote on the proposed amendment, and then the news would not be good for the religious right: The prayer-in-school amendment fell 11 votes shy of the two-thirds majority needed to move along in the process and was defeated.

THE ECONOMY WORSENS

As the second year of Reagan's presidency began, the economy grew worse. By July 1982, the poverty rate rose higher than it had been since 1967, increasing to 14 percent. Similarly, unemployment was higher in 1982 than it had been in the past 40 years, hitting 10.8 percent with more than 9 million Americans out of work by the end of the year. More than 25,000 businesses failed. In addition, interest rates on homes and cars

President Reagan discusses his tax and economic policies.
(Ronald Reagan Library)

rose, and the number of business bankruptcies and farm foreclosures increased to levels not seen since the Great Depression of the 1930s. Despite Reagan's promises to cut taxes, not raise them, Congress approved a tax increase of $98.3 billion in August 1982. Americans voiced their unhappiness with the state of the union by voting 26 Democrats into seats held by Republicans in the 1982 mid-term elections.

Reagan was also a proponent of deregulation, which became apparent during his presidency when his administration cut the budgets of many regulatory agencies. These groups also found their power weakened, their regulations ignored, and in some cases, new players from within their respective industries administering policy. Deregulation affected the policies of the Environmental Protection Agency, the Food and Drug Administration, the Department of Transportation, and the Department of the Interior.

As a result of deregulation, Reagan signed a bill in 1982 allowing savings and loan institutions to expand their market as it had been defined by federal regulations. Traditionally, savings and loans institutions provided low-yield savings accounts protected in part by the FDIC, and low-interest home and auto loans. The

Perhaps the most famous—and laughable—aspect of the proposed budget and services cuts was the Department of Agriculture's proposal that the condiments ketchup and pickle relish be considered vegetables in federally subsidized school lunches. After much criticism, the proposal was discarded.

In September 1982, Gannett began production of a national daily newspaper, *USA Today*. A colorful paper filled with graphs and charts, the paper offered highlights of national and international news, sports, leisure, business, and nationwide weather. Within four years, the periodical boasted 1 million readers, and newspapers nationwide were copying its style.

deregulation allowed savings and loan institutions to offer higher interest rates, and to make much riskier—sometimes worthless—investments with their customers' money. By 1985, the industry began to collapse. Exactly four years later, 350 savings and loans institutions had failed. Taxpayers ended up paying the $500 billion tab to repay the customers whose federally guaranteed funds were lost. Almost 150 of the failed institutions were located in Texas, while the majority of the others were in New England.

Deregulation also allowed Secretary of the Interior James Watt to offer the Pacific coastline to oil companies for drilling and exploration. Watt opposed additional environmental regulations and relaxed restrictions that had been imposed. Mining and timber companies also benefited from his lax regulations. Public outcry over Watt's policies led to his 1983 resignation.

FOREIGN AFFAIRS IN THE MIDDLE EAST

The Middle East was a hotbed of unrest in the 1980s. In June 1981, Israel destroyed an Iraqi nuclear reactor in order to keep that country from producing plutonium. Iran was rocked by the multiple deaths of political leaders and their aides by grenade attack and bombs in summer and fall 1981.

The Reagan administration stood firm on August 19, 1981, when two American military planes ventured over the Gulf of Sidrah, considered by Libya to be an official boundary line and by the United States to be international territory. Libya dispatched two fighter jets that were destroyed by the Americans. Less than a year later, on March 10, 1982, the United States called for an embargo against Libyan oil in retaliation against Libyan leader Muammar al-Qadhafi's alleged support of international terrorism.

On October 6, 1981, Egyptian president Anwar Sadat was assassinated by Muslim extremists in Cairo.

HEALING THE WOUNDS OF VIETNAM

On May 6, 1981, 21-year old Yale architecture student Maya Ying Lin's design was chosen from more than 1,400 entries by a jury of architects and sculptors to be the Vietnam Veterans Memorial. The memorial was meant to be nonpolitical and to help heal the wounds that had divided the nation during and after the Vietnam War. Lin's design featured a wall consisting of 140 polished black granite panels in a "v" formation, inscribed with the names of the 58,000 military personnel who perished in Vietnam between 1959 and 1975 or were still considered missing in action. More than 650,000 people contributed a total of $5 million to build the memorial, which was dedicated on Veterans' Day in 1982. Millions of people visited the memorial after its opening, many leaving flowers, letters, photos, clothing, and other mementos to loved ones who never returned home.

Yale architecture student Maya Ying Lin's design for the Vietnam Veterans Memorial was selected from more than 1,400 entries submitted. *(National Park Service)*

Sadat had worked with Israeli prime minister Menachem Begin and President Jimmy Carter at the Camp David Accords to bring peace to the Middle East. Sadat and Begin had received the 1978 Nobel Peace Prize for their work.

Egyptian president Anwar Sadat was assassinated by extremists on October 6, 1981. *(Jimmy Carter Library)*

In August 1982, the United States deployed Marines to Beirut, Lebanon. The U.S. troops were dispatched at Lebanon's request following an Israeli invasion of the country, which was torn by civil war. Although the 1,400 troops were withdrawn from Lebanon after the Palestinian Liberation Organization (PLO) left Beirut, they returned to the city after Lebanese president-elect Bashir Gemayel was killed when a bomb exploded on September 14, and Christians massacred Palestinians in refugee camps on September 16.

ECONOMIC AID TO THE CARIBBEAN

Just as Reagan feared Cuban, and therefore Soviet, influence would spread throughout Central America, he was also concerned about the same influence in the Caribbean. On February 24, 1982, President Reagan announced the Caribbean Basin Initiative (CBI), a policy that combined economic aid with security in order to combat the Cuban influence in that region. The CBI advocated one-way free trade for specific products from the region with the intent of promoting economic development and investment in those countries and securing the region from communism.

The military exercise "Ocean Venture 81" brought more than 120,000 troops, 1,000 aircraft, and 250 warships to the Caribbean. *(DOD Defense Visual Information Center)*

The U.S. military also engaged in exercises in the Caribbean, most notably "Ocean Venture 81" in August 1981. Held near Puerto Rico, this exercise involved more than 120,000 troops, 1,000 aircraft and 250 warships. This initiative also included Operation Amber, an exercise that the United States denied was a rehearsal for the Grenada invasion in 1983.

EL SALVADOR AND NICARAGUA

In 1981, Reagan repealed $75 million in aid for Nicaragua as a result of a State Department study that claimed that the country had supplied arms to Salvadoran rebels. The paper also held that rebels supported by Cuba had gone against the government of El Salvador, which the United States supported. Reagan also proposed providing $25 million in military aid to El Salvador, as well as military advisers. Leftists boycotted the 1982 elections, which therefore were won by the right wing. Military aid to El Salvador continued despite the American ambassador's requests to suspend it.

As the U.S. economy continued to struggle, the Reagan administration adhered to the so-called Reagan Doctrine, which sought to actively aid democratic revolutions and subvert the rise of communism, particularly in countries close to the United States. On November 23, 1981, Reagan signed National Security Decision Directive 17 (NSDD-17) authorizing $19 million in funding, as well as manpower, for the Central Intelligence Agency (CIA) to aid the Contras, a militia attempting to overthrow the Sandinistas, the ruling regime in Nicaragua. The Sandinistas had taken control of the Nicaraguan government in 1979, but radicals in the group soon assumed power, instituted socialist policies, and strengthened ties with communist countries.

In fact, in April 1981, the United States had suspended aid to Nicaragua because of the Sandinista

An estimated 750,000 protesters gathered in New York City's Central Park as a result of a special United Nations session on disarmament on June 12, 1982, in support of the nuclear freeze movement.

America's most trusted newsman, Walter Cronkite, retired from the *CBS Evening News* on March 6, 1981, after 19 years on the air.

regime's activities, in particular their alleged smuggling of weapons to El Salvadorean leftist rebels. NSDD-17 marked the first official support of the Contras by the United States. The Boland Amendment, passed by Congress on December 8, 1982, banned any assistance—including the supply of weapons and any training by the CIA—to groups attempting to overthrow the Sandinista government. This ban, however, would not deter the Reagan administration from supporting the Nicaraguan guerilla force in the future.

ARMS NEGOTIATIONS

On June 29, 1982, Strategic Arms Reductions Talks (START) between the United States and the Soviet Union began in Geneva. The United States proposed a reduction of strategic ballistic missile warheads and limited deployed strategic ballistic missiles to 850 both for themselves and the Soviets. The summit was inconclusive but did lay the groundwork for later negotiations.

While many considered Reagan to be pro-nuclear arms and confrontational, he was, in fact pro-disarmament. Reagan did not believe in the principle of mutually assured destruction (MAD), which held that the knowledge that each superpower had the ability to destroy the other kept the relationship in check. Reagan's intent was to overwhelm the Soviets with an extensive military buildup, making it too expensive for their struggling economy to keep up.

TELEVISION

When the primetime soap opera *Dynasty* debuted on January 12, 1981, no one could have imagined how well it would represent the 1980s. Everything about the show was larger than life, from the shoulder pads to the jewelery to the storylines. While the United States struggled through the recession of the early 1980s, the wealthy Carringtons and their cohorts lived large, and Americans wanted to emulate them.

Meanwhile, at the Southfork ranch, the trials and tribulations of the Ewing family continued on *Dallas*. *Hill Street Blues,* which debuted in 1981, included multiple plots involving a large cast of characters in each episode. *Hill Street Blues* and other dramatic ensemble shows appealed to an upscale demographic that was favored by advertisers.

For comic relief, Americans turned to *The Jeffersons, The Dukes of Hazzard, Alice,* and *Three's Company.* Old favorites *M*A*S*H* and *60 Minutes* remained in the top 10 both in 1981 and 1982. *Taxi* and *Cheers* were well established in the Thursday night lineup by fall 1982. While *60 Minutes* set high standards for serious reporting, the tabloid news program *Entertainment Tonight* premiered on September 14, 1981. The show celebrated show business, celebrities, and gossip, and it used high-tech graphics, elements that were soon adapted by regular television news programs.

"I WANT MY MTV!"

While the big three networks (ABC, CBS, and NBC) had traditionally dominated television, a new cable channel, was flying high. MTV (Music Television) debuted on August 1, 1981, at 12:01 A.M. with an airing of the Buggles' "Video Killed the Radio Star." The new channel showed video clips of songs—already an increasingly popular medium in Europe and Australia. Hosted by five veejays, video disc jockeys, the channel embraced a rock and roll format but relied largely on new bands that received little mainstream radio airplay to provide material.

Young people loved MTV; older people either hated it or were indifferent to it. The channel ultimately, however, became a huge factor in the success of many superstars of the 1980s, including Michael Jackson

Hit singles in 1981–82 included "Jessie's Girl" by Rick Springfield, "We Got the Beat" by the Go-Go's, "I Love Rock 'n' Roll" by Joan Jett and the Blackhearts, and "Open Arms" by Journey. *(Michele L. Camardella)*

WEDDINGS OF THE DECADE

On July 29, 1981, the wedding of Lady Diana Spencer and Prince Charles drew 600,000 spectators to the streets of London and over 750 million television viewers worldwide. Lacking their own royal family, millions of Americans were transfixed by the fairytale romance and spectacular pageantry. They were awestruck as Diana, a well-bred 20-year old kindergarten teacher, traveled to St. Paul's Cathedral in the Cinderella-esque glass coach, walked down the aisle with her 25-foot train trailing behind her, and exchanged vows with the 32-year-old heir to the British throne.

Just four months later, Americans enjoyed the next best thing to their own royal wedding when 30 million viewers watched the long-awaited wedding of Luke Spencer (Tony Geary) and Laura Webber-Baldwin (Genie Francis) on the daytime soap opera General Hospital. The episode, aired on November 16 and 17, 1981, had more viewers than any other in daytime soap opera history.

Cats opened on Broadway on October 7, 1982, beginning a run that would last until September 10, 2000.

and Madonna. Videos and a performer's image became as important as the songs themselves. Not only were bands and performers under pressure to look better then ever, but the videos were constantly improving and changing the face of the medium. Michael Jackson helped push the envelope regarding videos. His 1982 hit album *Thriller* spawned three hit videos, "Billie Jean," "Beat It," and the mini-movie "Thriller," which reportedly cost $1.1 million.

A year after its initial debut, MTV became available in Los Angeles and Manhattan, influencing music from coast to coast. The channel's advertising campaign, which featured rock stars like Sting of the rock band The Police and singer Cyndi Lauper admonishing, "I want my MTV!" was innovative, catchy, and a huge success. The medium was becoming more and more popular, and videos by bands like Flock of Seagulls, Men at Work, and the Stray Cats were being taken seriously as their impact on record sales was realized.

In the music world, the Go-Go's, an all-girl rock 'n' roll band, hit the charts with the infectious tunes "We Got the Beat" and "Our Lips Are Sealed." Punk-influenced Joan Jett and the Blackhearts scored with "I Love Rock 'n' Roll." Journey blanketed the airwaves with their ballad "Open Arms," and Diana Ross declared her "Endless Love" for Lionel Richie in their hit duet. Kim Carnes sang about a woman with "Bette Davis Eyes," while the J. Geils

VALLEY GIRLS

Although the name "Valley Girl" was initially coined in the 1970s to describe a girl who lived in California's San Fernando Valley, it took on a life of its own in the 1980s. The stereotypical Valley Girl lived to shop at the mall with her friends, where they stocked up on the latest fashions and makeup. Soon, young women across the country were wearing the decorated denim jackets and mini-skirts that every Valley Girl lived in. Even more prevalent was so-called Val speak. Teenage conversations were dominated by slang like "Barf me out," "Like, totally," "Fer sure," "I'm so sure," "Grody to the max," and "So bitchen!" In 1982, 14-year-old Moon Unit Zappa, daughter of experimental muscian Frank Zappa, captured the slang and gave the phenomenon even more momentum with the Top 40 single "Valley Girl."

Mall style ruled in the 1980s. This young woman is sporting stirrup pants, a high ponytail, and an off-the-shoulder top, all popular in the early to mid-1980s. *(Levis)*

Band imagined a high school sweetheart as a "Centerfold." Sheena Easton took the "Morning Train," Rick Springfield pined for "Jessie's Girl," and Olivia Newton-John topped the charts with "Physical."

FILM

Director Steven Spielberg struck box office gold in both 1981 and 1982, first with *Raiders of the Lost Ark* then with *E.T. the Extra-Terrestrial*. *Raiders* starred Harrison Ford as a daredevil archaeologist battling the Nazis in a quest for the Ark of the Covenant, a mythical object believed to be extremely powerful. In *E.T.,* Henry Thomas played a young boy who befriends a lovable alien who is trying to return to his home planet. The film grossed $228 million at the box office and set new standards in merchandising.

Other films in 1981 ranged from the teen sex farce *Porky's* to the star-studded Burt Reynold's vehicle *Cannonball Run* to the finely crafted *On Golden Pond,* starring Henry Fonda and Katharine Hepburn as a couple in their twilight years. Dudley Moore starred as the lovable drunk *Arthur,* and Bill Murray and friends took a comedic look at army life in *Stripes.*

On March 5, 1982, *Saturday Night Live* veteran and Blues Brother John Belushi died of a drug overdose at age 33.

Screen legend Henry Fonda, starred with daughter Jane Fonda (left) and Katharine Hepburn (right) in *On Golden Pond,* for which he won an Academy Award. *(AP/Wide World Photos)*

On September 14, 1982, former American screen star Princess Grace of Monaco (aka Grace Kelly) perished in a car accident.

Stand-out films from 1982 included Meryl Streep's heart-wrenching depiction of a Holocaust survivor in *Sophie's Choice,* Harrison Ford as an android hunter in the futuristic *Blade Runner,* and Dustin Hoffman as an actor so desperate for work that he masquerades as a woman to get a role in *Tootsie.* Ben Kingsley embodied Mohandas Gandhi in the film *Gandhi.* Though vastly different in terms of content, both *Diner* and *Fast Times at Ridgemont High* featured talented young casts that would go on to great fame. Kevin Bacon, Paul Reiser, Mickey Rourke, and Ellen Barkin were among the stars of *Diner,* while *Fast Times* featured Jennifer Jason Leigh, Phoebe Cates, Judge Reinhold, and Sean Penn, as well as Eric Stoltz and Anthony Edwards.

SPORTS

On December 11, 1981, legendary boxer Muhammad Ali retired following a loss to Trevor Berbick. For 21 years Ali had wowed both his fans and critics with his technique, power, and personality. He won 56 fights, 37 by knockout, and lost only 5 bouts, with just one by knockout. Ali would be hard to replace, but Sugar Ray Leonard attempted to do just that. During the 1980s, the fleet-footed Leonard won five world titles spanning five weight classes.

Baseball fans felt shortchanged when players went on strike for seven weeks in 1981. A staggering 713 games were cancelled in the middle of the season. In 1982, National Football League players went on strike for 57 days leaving fans in a lurch. Half of the 224 scheduled games were cancelled, and losses to owners, players, businesses, networks, and others totaled approximately $450 million.

In June 1981, Los Angeles Lakers' player Magic Johnson made history by signing a 25-year contract for $1 million per year, a new record in professional sports. The New York Yankees lost the World Series to the Los Angeles Dodgers despite being up two games to none initially. Dodgers' pitcher Fernando Valenzuela became the first player to win both the National League Cy Young award and the National League Rookie of the Year award in the same season. The New York Islanders won their third consecutive Stanley Cup.

As for personal fitness, aerobics classes were all the rage. The classes featured fast-paced exercises set to music and led by an instructor. Actress Jane Fonda found a second career as a fitness guru with the *Jane Fonda Workout Book* and a best-selling workout video. Perhaps it was more the workout-wear than the exercise that attracted so many followers. Leotards, tights, leg warmers, and headbands in vibrant colors and patterns became a part of everyday attire.

SCIENCE AND MEDICINE

As 1981 came to a close, Americans were awed by the birth of Elizabeth Jordan Carr, the first American test-tube baby. The world's first test-tube baby, Louise Brown, had been born in England three years earlier. Still, to many, the technology was new and fascinating. In vitro fertilization called for the removal of eggs from a woman's body, which were then fertilized with male sperm in a laboratory dish, and reinserted into the uterus of the woman or a surrogate who would carry the baby.

The year 1981 also marked the advent of acquired immune deficiency syndrome (AIDS). The disease had first appeared in young gay men in New York in March 1981 in the form of Kaposi's sarcoma, a rare cancer. At the same time, in both Los Angeles and New York, others were being diagnosed with the extremely rare

The first U.S. space shuttle was launched on April 12, 1981. The *Columbia* orbited Earth 36 times in 54 hours before returning to Earth. With the space shuttle designed to make as many as 100 flights, the launch marked a new era in space travel.

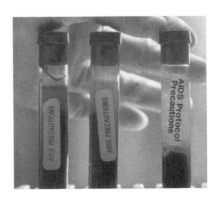

AIDS researchers wore rubber gloves and used protective measures while working.
(National Institutes of Health)

PAC MAN FEVER

In 1982, Americans spent countless hours and more than $5 billion in video arcades playing games like Pac Man, Space Invaders, and Asteroids. Americans were also obsessed—and frustrated—with the Rubik's Cube, a multicolored cube-shaped puzzle. An estimated 100 million Rubik's Cubes were sold worldwide between 1980 and 1982, in addition to the cheaper knockoff puzzles that were readily available.

Millions of people worldwide were frustrated by the Rubik's Cube puzzle. *(The reproduction of this image is by kind permission of Seven Towns Limited www.rubiks.com.)*

Pneumocystis carinii pneumonia (PCP), a condition that only exists when there is an impaired immune system. By November 1982, AIDS cases had been reported in 33 countries.

While many of the victims were gay, others were intravenous drug users, an indication that the disease was not confined to the homosexual community. Eventually, it was discovered that AIDS was transferred via the exchange of body fluids. Initially, many people reacted to AIDS with hysteria; parents refused to let their children attend classes with AIDS victims, rumors circulated that it was possible to contract the disease from a toilet seat, and many with the disease were shunned by the world at large and even by their own families. An average of 10 new AIDS diagnoses were made each week during 1982, and the disease would be deemed an epidemic later in the decade. Perhaps because of the distaste that the religious right held for the homosexual lifestyle, the Reagan administration was slow to react to the AIDS crisis.

TECHNOLOGY

Technology made life infinitely easier for businesses in the early 1980s. In 1981, IBM introduced its first personal computer (PC), which ran the Microsoft Disk Operating System (MS-DOS) and used the Intel 8088 microprocessor. The IBM PC became the most popular computer in the world. In 1982, additional technology made facsimile (fax) machines more efficient, increasing their importance in the workplace as well. Such modern technology brought about huge changes in offices, allowing information to be created and shared quickly and easily.

CHAPTER 3

A ROLLER-COASTER ECONOMY, 1983–1984

I N 1983–84, THE U.S. ECONOMY WAS A roller coaster, with a decline in both unemployment and interest rates, and an increase in housing and automobile sales. In fact in mid-1984, American automobile company profits hit new heights. Yet in 1983, 11.5 million people were unemployed, a number that would increase threefold by the end of the year. The following year, the unemployment rate fell to 7.4 percent. The inflation rate, meanwhile, which was 11.2 percent when Reagan took office, dipped to 3.2 percent in 1983, and rose to 4.3 percent the following year.

In his address at the Annual Convention of the National Association of Evangelicals on March 8, 1983, President Reagan referred to the Soviet Union as an "evil empire."
(Ronald Reagan Library)

NUCLEAR FEARS

Nuclear war was on the minds of many Americans in the early 1980s. A controversial made-for-television movie entitled *The Day After* depicted the aftermath of a nuclear war and was seen by approximately 1 million viewers.

After viewing the show, undergraduate students at Brown University voted to have the health service stock pills that would be available for student suicides in the case of nuclear attack.

Fearing the eventual depletion of funds, the Reagan administration tackled the issue of Social Security, the financial safety net for America's senior citizens. Through the Social Security Reform act of 1983, Congress approved the gradual increase of the full retirement age to 67 for those born in or after 1960. Other existing benefits were cancelled or became taxable. The act was implemented with the intent of keeping Social Security viable for another 75 years.

Unfortunately, any positive trends in the economy were countered by record increase in the federal deficit, thanks to large tax cuts and increased defense spending. In 1983, the poverty rate hit 15.2 percent, the highest in almost 20 years. Essentially, this meant that there were 6 million more people living in poverty in 1983 than there were when Reagan assumed office. This particularly affected the urban and working poor and contributed greatly to the growing problem of homelessness. By 1984, the federal deficit had more than doubled to $185 billion, and the savings that had been recognized by cutting numerous domestic programs were negated by the interest payments on the debt. As Reagan's second term began, he proposed another $100 billion in budget cuts.

Peace rallies and protests against nuclear weapons and power were prevalent in the early 1980s. This No Nukes rally took place at Swarthmore College. *(Theodore Hetzel Collection, Swarthmore College Peace Collection)*

PRAYER AND THE PRESIDENT

Although Reagan remained soft on many issues that were dear to the religious right, he still courted their vote. In fact, the day he accepted his party's nomination as their candidate for the 1984 election, he was in Dallas, Texas, at a prayer breakfast with 17,000 supporters.

One issue that Reagan did support was a constitutional amendment requiring prayer in public school. Although the legislation garnered a majority of votes, 56-44, it failed to secure the necessary quorum by 11 votes and did not pass in the Senate.

BUILDING A STRONGER AMERICA

In 1982, Reagan announced a five-year plan that included $1.2 trillion for defense spending. This figure, however, did not include the hundreds of billions of dollars that would later be estimated as the cost of the Strategic Defense Initiative (SDI), also known as Star Wars. This controversial anti-missile program was meant to defend the United States from both land and space. Believing that the Soviet Union had surpassed the United States in military might, Reagan held that the program would help keep peace. He also contended that America would share the yet-undeveloped technology as the program, which used lasers and depended largely on computers, was developed. SDI's greatest fault was that nuclear weapons had to be launched to test it. Although the program was never completely abandoned, its scope and allocated budget were greatly downscaled over the years. Still, by 1988, over $12 billion had been committed to the project.

In December 1983, the Soviet Union walked out of the Intermediate Nuclear Forces (INF) talks in response to the development of SDI. They also abandoned the Strategic Arms Reduction Talks (START). In addition, after just 15 months in office, Soviet general secretary Yuri Andropov died in February 1984 and was succeeded by his rival, Konstantin Chernenko. Later that year, in September, Soviet Foreign Minister Andrei

In 1983, Chrysler introduced the new minivan, as an alternative to the family-friendly station wagon. In their first year on the market, half a million minivans were sold, which saved Chrysler from impending bankruptcy. Chrysler's amazing turnaround also made its chairman, Lee Iacocca, a household name.

Gromyko traveled to Washington, D.C., in an attempt to reopen communication with the Reagan administration regarding arms issues, which resulted in Reagan's agreement to begin talks again in 1985.

THE 1984 PRESIDENTIAL CAMPAIGN AND ELECTION

Walter Mondale, the former Minnesota senator who served as vice president under Jimmy Carter, was nominated as the Democratic candidate for the 1984 presidential election. Other Democratic candidates for the nomination included: Senator John Glenn (Ohio), who in 1962 became the first astronaut to orbit the Earth; Senator Gary Hart (Colorado), often compared to John F. Kennedy; Senator Alan Cranston (California), whose major platform focus was arms control and nuclear freeze issues; and the Reverend Jesse Jackson, a leader in the civil rights movement and the first black man to be considered seriously as a presidential hopeful. The Democratic Party also made history by being the first major party to nominate a woman as vice

President Reagan debated his opponent, former vice president Walter Mondale, in the 1984 presidential campaign. *(Ronald Reagan Library)*

President Reagan embarked on a whistle stop tour during the 1984 presidential campaign. *(Ronald Reagan Library)*

President Reagan and Vice President Bush wave to the crowd at the 1984 Republican convention. *(Ronald Reagan Library)*

president. Geraldine Ferraro, a Congresswoman from New York, joined Mondale on the ticket.

Reagan was at the height of his popularity in 1984, and Mondale's promise to raise taxes in order to lower the federal deficit was not a popular position. Mondale's strategy was to appeal to traditionally Democratic groups such as the AFL-CIO, women's organizations, and civil rights groups, which led to the accusation that he was catering to special interest groups like unions, teachers, and minorities. The president's $1.8 million campaign budget featuring the slogan "Morning in America," overwhelmed Mondale. On November 6, 1984, Reagan won 59 percent of the popular vote, and 525 Electoral College votes—more than any other presidential candidate in history. He managed to cross a variety of age and cultural boundaries, winning the vote of men and women, the young and the elderly, Catholics and Jews, and even union households. Mondale won only his home state of Minnesota and the District of Columbia.

Despite failing to regain the presidency in 1984, the Democratic Party gained seats in both the Senate and the

Congresswoman Geraldine Ferraro, seen here debating vice president George Bush, was the first female vice presidential candidate on a major party ticket. *(George Bush Presidential Library)*

President and Mrs. Reagan view the flag-draped caskets of U.S. Marines who perished in the Beirut bombing. *(Ronald Reagan Library)*

House or Representatives in the 1986 Congressional elections. In addition, Democratic candidate for vice president Geraldine Ferraro made history by being the first woman from a major party to run for national office.

LOSSES IN LEBANON

American troops were dispatched to Beirut, Lebanon, in the early 1980s, following an Israeli invasion of the country, which was torn by civil war. In April 1983, 47 people were killed when a car bombed exploded outside the U.S. Embassy. On May 17, 1983, Lebanon, Israel, and the United States signed an agreement regarding Israel's withdrawal from Lebanon, but the agreement failed to have any staying power. In August and September of that year, U.S. Marines died in attacks by Muslim groups, leading to an order from Reagan for U.S. warships to take action against Muslim positions. On October 23, 1983, the United States suffered a devastating loss when a Muslim terrorist suicide bomber drove a pickup truck filled with explosives into a building filled with sleeping Marines, killing 241 and wounding 115. The attack also killed 58 French paratroopers. The United States removed the remaining Marines from Lebanon in February 1984.

THE INVASION OF GRENADA

On October 19, 1983, the prime minister of Grenada, Maurice Bishop, and others in his cabinet were executed in a military coup, or an overthrow of the government. The following day, Vice President Bush, Secretary of State Shultz, and the National Security Council met and decided to redirect the aircraft carrier the USS *Independence* from its course toward Lebanon to Grenada. This was done to ensure the safety of nearly 1,000 Americans living on this island—700 of them students at St. George's University School of Medicine. At the request of the leaders of the Organisation of Eastern Caribbean States (OECS), the United States took over the leadership and organization of the invasion of Grenada in conjunction with a multinational force including personnel from six Caribbean countries: Antigua, Barbados, Dominica, Jamaica, St. Lucia, and St. Vincent.

Operation Urgent Fury went into effect on Tuesday, October 25, when elite U.S. Navy SEALS began their attempts to secure the governor general's residence. Shortly thereafter, 400 Marines in armed helicopters landed at Pearls Airport, and 800 U.S. Army Rangers

American medical students wait to board a plane for evacuation from Grenada as U.S. servicemen look on. *(DOD Defense Visual Information Center)*

"Where's the beef?"

—Clara Peller, in commercials for Wendy's fast food restaurants

parachuted into Point Salinas Airport. While the Marines faced little anti-aircraft fire, the Rangers were confronted with considerable anti-aircraft fire, allegedly from Cubans working at the airport. Within hours of the invasion 600 Cubans were captured and placed under the guard of Caribbean troops. The next day, American medical students were evacuated from one campus, while those at a second campus had to wait for one more day as U.S. forces faced the Grenadian army. The second group experienced a more dramatic beach-front rescue by helicopter that involved some crossfire.

Final figures from each side vary, and many believe that the number of Grenadian dead was underestimated. Combined figures indicate 18 U.S. military casualties, 24 Cuban military casualties, and 16 Grenadian military casualties. In addition, 113 Americans, 57 Cubans, and 280 Grenadians were wounded.

The American position in Grenada was not widely supported internationally; 79 governments made public statements expressing their disapproval of U.S. activities within the week following the invasion. The United States immediately granted $3 million in aid to Grenada, whose economy had been decimated. Eventually, an additional $20 million in aid would be committed to various initiatives, particularly for the development of better road and water systems and to station health and education personnel. In addition, the United States managed to expel from Grenada all diplomats from the Soviet Union, eastern Europe, and Libya, as well as the majority of personnel at the Cuban embassy. Hundreds of army engineers and other specialists remained in Grenada after American combat troops withdrew in early December 2003.

Although Reagan ordered the invasion without the consent of Congress, which is the only body that has the power to declare war according to the U.S. Constitution, the circumstances were never investigated. Congress did, however, vote to apply the War Powers

resolution to ensure that unless Congress approved continued deployment, the troops had to return home after 60 days.

THE IRAN-CONTRA AFFAIR

In October 1984, Congress adopted the second Boland Amendment, which terminated all assistance to the Nicaraguan Contras. The Reagan administration interpreted the amendment as a ban on intelligence agency support, but not on aid from the National Security Council (NSC). The Reagan administration sought more support for the initiative, resulting in a compromise in early December 1983, when funding for the Contras was capped at $24 million for the 1984 fiscal year. This amount was far lower than the funding that the administration desired, and they retained the option to approach Congress for additional funds at a later date. When it was discovered that the CIA had

President Reagan's second cabinet, photographed in 1984, included William Casey (third row, sixth from left), director of the CIA during the Iran-Contra affair, and Ed Meese (third row, seventh from left), who was eventually appointed special prosecutor to look into the Iran-Contra scandal. Other important administration officials pictured include (first row, left to right) Donald Regan, secretary of the Treasury; Vice President Bush; President Reagan; George Shultz, secretary of state; and Caspar Weinberger, secretary of defense. *(Ronald Reagan Library)*

Don Johnson (left) and Phillip Michael Thomas's colorful T-shirts and unstructured jackets worn in the television show *Miami Vice* greatly influenced men's fashion in the mid-1980s. *(Kobal Collection)*

FASHION

In the 1980s, fashion trends were heavily influenced by movies, television shows, and celebrities. *Flashdance* prompted an off-the-shoulder sweatshirt and leg warmer fad. Madonna's habit of wearing lingerie as clothing started a new trend, as did her black rubber bracelets.

secretly mined Nicaraguan harbors in April 1984, Congress refused additional funding. The CIA also bombed Nicaraguan oil refineries, provided assassination manuals to the Contras, and advised them on how to destroy bridges and dams that had been built by the Army Corps of Engineers. The Contra support program was illegal, and its proponents soon sought funding outside Congress.

Early in 1984, National Security Advisor Robert C. McFarlane and William Casey, director of the CIA, agreed that it might be worthwhile to encourage other countries to support the Contras. The National Security Planning Group (NSPG), comprising the president, vice president, and several national security officials, considered such third-party funding. As early as May 1984, Saudi Arabia had agreed to make a monthly contribution of $1 million. Ultimately, Saudi Arabia contributed between $15 and $30 million to the Contras.

Instructed by the president to take over the illicit Contra support program from the CIA, NSC advisor McFarlane made Lieutenant Colonel Oliver North the coordinator of the covert war. McFarlane's assistant at the NSC, North was instructed to establish secret Swiss bank accounts for the Saudi Arabian funds. North also sought assistance from retired air force major general Richard Secord in purchasing arms for the Contras. Secord, in turn, pulled in Robert Owen, who met regularly with Contra leader Adolfo Calero to deliver funds and intelligence, and to determine what the rebels needed. CIA Central America Task Force Chief Alan Fiers and Assistant Secretary of State Elliott Abrams also ranked high in the Contra program.

EL SALVADOR

On May 25, 1983, rebel forces in El Salvador allegedly shot and killed Lieutenant Commander Albert A. Schaufelberger III, a U.S. military adviser. Nearly two weeks later, 100 U.S. Special Forces troops began training Salvadoran forces in Honduras. Although Congress approved $55 million in additional military aid to El Salvador, the amount was half of what was initially requested by the president. In addition, the aid was contingent upon progress being made in the area of human rights in El Salvador, a country in which more than 30,000 civilians were killed between 1979 and 1983. The following year, Congress approved a $500 million aid package for the country after the moderate Jose Napoleon Duarte won the national elections.

FILM

In 1984, the Motion Picture Association of America (MPAA) introduced the PG-13 rating, marking the first change to the movie ratings system since its inception in 1968. The new rating fell between PG (Parental Guidance) and R (Restricted) and was meant to inform parents that violence or other content might not be suitable for youngsters under the age of 14. *Red Dawn,* a film about eight teenagers who fight the Russians when they invade America during World War III, was the first film to be released with the new rating.

Return of the Jedi, the sequel to *Star Wars,* kept fans enthralled in 1983 while *The Big Chill* focused on college friends reuniting for a funeral as 30-somethings, all to a soundtrack of golden oldies. *Flashdance,* the tale of a woman who is a welder by day and a dancer by night, made off-the-shoulder sweatshirts and leg warmers fashionable. *Risky Business* catered to teenagers, featuring Tom Cruise as a college-bound senior who unexpectedly gets involved with a prostitute and her friends. Molly Ringwald, meanwhile, suffered teen angst as Samantha, whose family forgets her 16th birthday because they are too preoccupied with her older sister's impending wedding in *Sixteen Candles,* released in 1984. In many ways, these two films mark the beginning of

After 2,377 shows, the beloved Broadway musical *Annie* closed on January 2, 1983.

"I'll be back."
—Arnold Schwarzenegger as the cyborg in *The Terminator*

"Go ahead, make my day."
—Clint Eastwood as Harry Callahan in *Sudden Impact*

Comedian Andy Kaufman, best known as Latka Gravas on the sitcom *Taxi*, succumbed to cancer on May 16, 1984.

the so-called Brat Pack movies so prevalent throughout the 1980s.

Other films of 1984 included the award-winning *Amadeus,* the spooky comedy *Ghostbusters,* the political drama *The Killing Fields,* and the mock-documentary *This Is Spinal Tap,* which lovingly poked fun at the rock 'n' roll bands. The second installment of Spielberg's Indiana Jones adventure series, *Indiana Jones and the Temple of Doom,* was darker than the first film, but a hit nonetheless. Kevin Bacon danced his way through *Footloose* as a rebellious Chicago teen who moves to a rural town where music and dancing have been banned.

TELEVISION

Loyal viewers bid farewell to a long-running favorite series, *M*A*S*H.* In the episode entitled "Goodbye, Farewell, Amen," Hawkeye Pierce, Colonel Potter, Hot Lips Houlihan, B. J. Hunnicutt, Father Mulcahy, and Maxwell Klinger finally were able to return home as the war ended. More than 125 million Americans watched the episode and said good-bye to the beloved characters.

Left to right: Tempestt Bledsoe and Keshia Knight Pulliam played the young daughters of Bill Cosby and Phylicia Rashad in the immensely popular sitcom *The Cosby Show. (Kobal Collection)*

Meanwhile, comedian Bill Cosby scored a hit with *The Cosby Show.* The family sitcom featured Cosby as a doctor married to a lawyer and raising five children in a Brooklyn brownstone. Embraced by the public, the show finished third in the ratings in its debut season, and it remained in the number one spot for the next four years. The popular sitcom sparked discussion by depicting a highly successful upper-middle-class black family with traditional values.

After the acclaimed sitcom *Taxi* ended, Tony Danza scored a hit with *Who's the Boss,* in which he played a male housekeeper and single parent working in the suburban home of a female executive. The family comedy *Family Ties* also debuted in 1984, featuring Meredith Baxter-Birney and Michael Gross as aging hippie parents. Playing their super-conservative and greedy but good-hearted son, Michael J. Fox emerged as a star.

MUSIC

Bruce "The Boss" Springsteen released *Born in the U.S.A.* in 1984. The album produced seven Top 10 singles, and remained on the Top 40 album charts for almost two years following seven weeks at number one. Many people, including President Reagan, failed to recognize that Springsteen's album was not a glowing tribute to America, but rather a scathing criticism of the current state of affairs. The video for "Dancing in the Dark" proved to be a big break for Courtney Cox, playing the girl who is pulled from the audience to dance with the Boss. Cox went on to star as Alex's love interest in *Family Ties,* although she gained her greatest fame later as Monica on the sitcom *Friends* in the 1990s.

MTV continued to be a driving, evolving force in both television and music. By 1983, just two years after the network's launch, it boasted transmission to 14 million households. The next year, MTV had 22 million viewers. Artists whose videos appeared on MTV saw

The album *Born in the U.S.A.* by Bruce "The Boss" Springsteen spawned seven top-10 singles. *(Paul Natkin/Photo Reserve)*

Lionel Ritchie (above) is interviewed by MTV VJ Mark Goodman. Following the success of his 1985 *Dancing on the Ceiling* album, Lionel Ritchie became one of the few black artists in heavy rotation during MTV's early days. *(MTV)*

Madonna's over-the-top performance at the 1984 MTV Video Music Awards catapulted her to fame. *(Paul Natkin/Photo Reserve)*

On February 4, 1983, Karen Carpenter of the brother-sister pop duo The Carpenters died of complications from anorexia nervosa. The singer and drummer had battled the eating disorder for 15 years and was just 32 years old when her heart failed.

their record sales increase by as much as 15 to 20 percent. The following year, MTV began to charge record companies for airing their artists' videos. (Previously they were aired free of charge.) MTV's influence could also be felt in feature films like *Flashdance.*

In addition, the channel shared hip hop with the masses, introducing break dancing, graffiti, and street culture from the Bronx, New York, to the rest of America. Hip hop had been a largely underground phenomenon, thriving in urban areas. Mixing, sampling, and scratching were common elements of hip hop and rap. The DJ would place the turntable needle in the groove of a record and manually manipulate the turntable resulting in scratching. Hip hop also involved sampling borrowed pieces of other existing, usually popular songs, mixing them in with another song.

MTV was largely responsible for making Madonna a star. The pop-singer and dancer scored a hit with her second album *Like a Virgin,* especially with the title single, as well as "Material Girl," and "Dress You Up." But it was Madonna's performance at the 1984 MTV Video Music Awards that gained notoriety. Wearing a wedding dress and veil, and singing "Like a Virgin" as she

GAMES AND TOYS

More than 1 million copies of the game Trivial Pursuit were sold in America when it was released in 1983. The next year, 20 million units were sold, reinvigorating the board game industry. Cabbage Patch Dolls were the hot ticket during the 1983 holidays, as people lined up for hours outside toy stores hoping to take home a baby doll for their child. These cuddly, individualized dolls came with a name, birth certificate, and adoption papers. Over 3 million dolls were sold by the end of 1983, with sales of $60 million. The following year, robot figures, particularly Go-Bots and Transformers, were top sellers.

writhed around on the stage, Madonna broke all the rules of an awards show in a performance that catapulted her to fame.

In other popular music, the Greg Kihn Band lost in "Jeopardy," Australian band Men at Work made vegemite a household word in "Down Under," and Culture Club asked "Do You Really Want to Hurt Me?" Motley Crüe, Ratt, Twisted Sister, and Van Halen represented hard rock on the charts. Van Halen's *1984* featured the hits "Jump," "Panama," and "Hot for Teacher."

The Police released *Synchronicity*, which would be their last release as a working band. Billy Joel recorded an homage to doo-wop with *An Innocent Man.* The British bands Spandau Ballet and Duran Duran epitomized the new romantic movement—well-dressed and well-coifed bands that were the antithesis of punk rock. Chameleon David Bowie returned with a new look for *Let's Dance,* included the hits "China Girl," "Modern Love," and the title track.

In 1984, Bob Geldof of the Boomtown Rats organized the all-star Band Aid to record the single "Do They Know It's Christmas?" Sales of the single, which featured Midge Ure, Sting, David Bowie, Phil Collins, members of U2, Duran Duran, and Spandau Ballet, as well as others, benefited Ethiopian famine relief. Band Aid was the first of many all-star collaborations for charity that would continue throughout the 1980s.

Vanessa Williams announced her resignation as Miss America on July 23, 1984. It marked two firsts: Williams was the first black Miss America in the 63 year history of the pageant, as well as the first winner ever to resign her title.

1984: THE YEAR OF THE YUPPIE

An acronym for young, urban, upwardly mobile professionals, *yuppie* referred to those born between 1945 and 1964 that lived in cities, worked as professionals or managers, and earned over $40,000 annually. Yuppies thrived in Reagan's America, numbering approximately 1.5 million. They enjoyed buying expensive cars, cutting edge electronics, gourmet food, and designer clothes. In addition, they were regulars at health spas and indulged in pricey workout gear and sneakers. The decadence of yuppie lifestyle was captured in print in the novels *Bright Lights, Big City* by Jay McInerney, and *Less Than Zero* by Bret Easton Ellis. The stock market crash of October 19, 1987, ended the fun for many, and by 1988, the term *yuppie* was virtually considered a dirty word associated with greed and wanton excess.

SPORTS

The 1984 Winter Olympics were held in February in Sarajevo, Yugoslavia. American Scott Hamilton took the gold medal in men's figure skating. Brothers Phil and Steve Mahre won the gold and silver in men's Alpine slalom, while teammate Bill Johnson came in first in men's downhill skiing. By the end of the games, the United States ranked fifth in overall medals.

The 1984 Summer Olympics were held in Los Angeles. In May, just a few months prior to their start, the Soviet Union boycotted the games in retaliation against the United States–led boycott of the 1980 Moscow Summer Olympics. The USSR and 16 of its allies, with the exception of Romania, boycotted the games. Still, the Olympics provided excitement, with 168 hours of events aired. Mary Lou Retton, a 16-year-old gymnast, won five medals, including the gold for all-around performance. Carl Lewis duplicated Jesse Owens's feat in the 1936 Berlin Olympics, winning gold medals in the 100- and 200-meter dashes, the 400-meter relay, and the long jump. Overall, American athletes won 174 medals, including 83 gold medals.

A record 111.5 million viewers tuned in to watch the Washington Redskins beat the Miami Dolphins 27-17 in the Superbowl. In July 1983, Martina Navratilova won her fourth Wimbledon singles championship while John McEnroe won his second. Navratilova also won her first U.S. Open singles title in

On January 22, 1983, tennis champion Bjørn Bjorg retired after winning five consecutive Wimbledon championships.

September of that year. In April 1984, Kareem Abdul-Jabbar became the NBA's all-time scorer, breaking the record of 31,419 points held by Wilt Chamberlain. And after 14 years on the air, controversial sportscaster Howard Cosell quit *Monday Night Football.*

SCIENCE AND TECHNOLOGY

Astronaut Sally Ride's June 18, 1983, voyage on the *Challenger* space shuttle marked the first by an American woman. October 11, 1984, marked another first for a female American astronaut: Kathryn D. Sullivan performed a space walk. Earlier in 1984, astronauts Bruce McCandless II and Robert L. Stewart completed the first untethered space walk.

The compact disc (CD) was introduced in 1983. Portability, a greater capacity to store music, and durability made the new media extremely popular. In March 1983, Apple Computer debuted their Lisa model, which included a handheld electronic cursor control, or a mouse. The following January, Apple unveiled the

Astronaut Sally Ride was the first American woman to participate in a space shuttle mission. *(National Aeronautics and Space Administration, NASA)*

THE PC OFFICE

Early PCs featured glowing letters on a dark screen—no gray tones, colors, graphics, or pictures. *(IBM)*

The PC, or personal computer, became ubiquitous in business settings mainly because of the development of a financial spreadsheet application called VisiCalc in 1979. Later database and spreadsheet software based on VisiCalc, such as Lotus 1-2-3, was developed and refined throughout the 1980s. The spreadsheet programs became the so-called killer apps or necessary applications that led businesses to buy PCs in bulk.

Because these financial applications made accounting and data analysis faster than ever before, businesses had more accurate financial and inventory information, which let them run more efficiently and beat the competition. Soon, word processing programs were developed, which made computers even more essential in the office, as PCs replaced typewriters, and electronic data stored on discs or tape slowly began to take the place of file cabinets full of paper. They used large floppy discs to store small amounts of data of less than a megabyte. In contrast, a music CD stores just over 70 megabytes; iPods store thousands of CDs; and DVDs store gigabytes of data.

This Apple III model was the first to incorporate a built-in floppy disk drive. *(Apple Corp.)*

Dr. Robert Gallo led the research team that conducted groundbreaking research on the HIV virus. *(National Institutes of Health)*

Macintosh computer, which sold for $2,495. More expensive than its competitor, the IBM PC, the Mac featured a superior graphic interface. The same year, IBM introduced the IBM AT (Advanced Technology) PC, which was faster and had greater capabilities than the original PC. In addition, MS-DOS, the computer language developed for IBM by Microsoft, became hugely popular and was used in more than 2 million computers. Hewlett Packard also entered new terrain when they introduced the laptop computer in 1984.

THE AIDS CRISIS WORSENS

By 1983, it was apparent that AIDS was having a great impact in the United States. Misunderstanding about how the disease was transferred and who was at risk led to more fear and confusion. In March 1983, the Public Health Service recommended that those at risk to contract AIDS should not donate blood in order to calm fears about the disease being transmitted through blood transfusions. Although there was no evidence that donating blood was in any way a risk, donations fell 6 to 10 percent in 1983.

In August 1983, the most extensive Congressional hearings to date were held by a subcommittee on Intergovernmental Relations and Human Resources. The hearings led to a request for more proposed funding to research and combat AIDS. Despite the fact that the Center for Disease Control's (CDC) request for more funding had been denied, just two weeks after the hearings the proposed budget for AIDS research was raised from $17.6 million to $39 million. Perhaps more important the proceedings convinced many in Congress that the Reagan Administration was not taking this health crisis seriously. On April 23, 1984, it was announced that a research team led by Dr. Robert Gallo had determined that a virus caused AIDS, the first step toward developing effective treatments.

CHAPTER 4

REAGAN'S SECOND TERM, 1985–1986

Due to inclement weather, President Reagan was sworn in at a private ceremony in the White House on January 20, 1985, while a public ceremony (pictured) in the U.S. Capitol rotunda was held on January 21. *(Ronald Reagan Library)*

THE NEW YEAR IN THE WHITE HOUSE started with what some considered a strange turn of events. White House Chief of Staff James A. Baker and Treasury Secretary Donald T. Regan switched jobs on January 8, 1985, a swap orchestrated by Reagan aide Michael Deaver. On January 20, 1985, Ronald Wilson Reagan was sworn in as president for his second term. Frigid temperatures as low as two degrees below fahrenheit forced the outdoor ceremony to be moved inside to the grand foyer of the White House, and the cancellation of the traditional inaugural parade. Because the inauguration fell on a Sunday, Reagan was sworn in again on Monday in the Capitol rotunda. The president and first lady attended the nine inaugural balls that were held that evening.

THE DECLINE OF THE FAMILY FARM

Family farms faced a crisis in the mid-1980s as a result of soaring interest rates and falling land prices. Although Congress passed an $87 billion bill to offer relief to farmers, 43,000 farms went bankrupt in 1985. Between 1980 and 1985, farm debt increased 27 percent, topping $210 billion. By the early 1980s, the number of family farms had decreased in alarming numbers, from 6.5 million in 1930 to only 2 million in 1984. In 1985, Congress passed an $87 billion bill to offer relief to farmers.

THE DRUG CRISIS: "JUST SAY NO"

An estimated 40 million people in the United States used illegal drugs each year during the 1980s. Crack was introduced to the United States in 1985. In the next few years, crack use, a potent smokable form of cocaine became prevalent, particularly in urban areas. Crack houses, or locations where crack addicts congregated to get high and then recover, were commonplace in poor urban neighborhoods nationwide, as were violent crimes associated with the sale and use of the highly addictive drug. The surprising death of athlete Len Bias, a University of Maryland basketball player, from cocaine in June 1986 also called attention to the problems of drug use.

In August 1986, Reagan introduced six initiatives meant to reduce drug use: drug-free workplaces in the private and government sectors; drug-free schools; treatment availability; international cooperation regarding drug trafficking; strengthened law enforcement regarding drugs; and expansion of public awareness and drug use prevention. One month later, on September 16, 1986, during a television address to the nation the president and Mrs. Reagan introduced the Just Say No campaign, meant to deter young people from using drugs. The campaign became the first lady's public outreach vehicle during the Reagan presidency. The day after the address, Reagan called for $900 million to be earmarked for the war on drugs. Congress took

Crack, a potent form of cocaine, was introduced in the United States in 1986. (*Drug Enforcement Administration*)

his plan a step further, and passed a plan that almost doubled Reagan's original funding initiative. In October 1986, Congress passed and Reagan signed into law an antidrug program totaling $1.7 billion.

TAX REFORM

In 1985, Reagan introduced a comprehensive reform of the tax code meant to simplify taxes, lower them, and make them fairer. Initially, Reagan's plan called for three tax brackets, or levels of taxation, at 15, 25, and 35 percent of income. The plan also included an increase in the personal exemption and ended deductions for state and local taxes, as well as for interest payments with the exception of mortgages. In December 1985, Reagan even visited Capitol Hill, which a sitting president rarely does, to show his support for the tax reform bill.

Both the House and the Senate worked on their own tax reform plans using Reagan's proposal as a guide; the two measures were then combined. Ultimately, the tax brackets were reduced to 2, 15, and 31 percent, to be phased in over time. In addition, the personal exemption and standard deductions were increased. Deductions for state and local taxes, as well as interest payments for credit cards and other itemized

First Lady Nancy Reagan embraced drug use prevention as her pet cause, embarking on the Just Say No campaign on September 16, 1986. *(Ronald Reagan Library)*

MULTIMILLIONAIRES BEHIND BARS

In the mid-1980s, some of America's financial wizards hit rock bottom, the two best known being Ivan Boesky and Michael Millken. Boesky ran Ivan F. Boesky and Company in New York, as well as Cambrian & General Securities based in London. He made his fortune purchasing securities and selling them immediately in another market and making a profit from the price discrepancy. Boesky was indicted on charges of insider trading, or acting on information not available to the public to buy and sell securities, in 1986. He became an informant for the Securities and Exchange Commission and paid $100 million in fines in exchange for serving a sentence of only two years in federal prison. He also lost his right to ever trade American securities again. Similarly, Michael Millken was indicted for fraud and racketeering in 1987. A senior vice president at Drexel Burnham, Millken had used junk bonds, which are rated below investment grade and are considered to be high risk, as a means to finance corporate takeovers. In 1988, Millken pleaded guilty to improper trading, and received a sentence of 10 years and a $600 million fine.

Vice President George H. W. Bush served as acting president for eight hours on July 13, 1985, while Reagan underwent surgery to remove a malignant colon polyp.

President and Mrs. Reagan wave from the window of Bethesda Naval Hospital, where the president underwent various procedures. *(Ronald Reagan Library)*

deductions were eliminated. The Tax Reform Act of 1986 was signed into law by President Reagan on October 22, 1986.

CONGRESS IN THE SECOND TERM

The economy forced Congress to take action on the budget deficit. Exports decreased slightly between 1980 and 1985, while imports to the United States increased 41 percent, resulting in increased trade deficits. By the end of 1985, the budget deficit was nearing more than $200 billion, a mark it surpassed in 1986. On December 11, 1985, Congress passed the Gramm-Rudman-Hollings Act, or the Balanced Budget and Emergency Deficit Control Act of 1985. This act allowed for automatic spending cuts to be implemented in the event that the president and Congress failed to agree on a balanced federal budget and sought to eliminate the federal deficit by October 1, 1990. Inflation averaged 3.5 percent in 1985 and dipped below 2 percent the following year, a welcome respite from previous years. The unemployment figures hovered around 7 percent in 1985 and 1986.

Perhaps due to public dissatisfaction with congressional action on unemployment, Democrats gained seats in the November 1986 elections and assumed control of the Senate. At the same time, however, eight Republican governors won their races, including those in Texas and Florida, traditionally Democratic states. In addition, Reagan appointed an associate justice to the Supreme Court in 1986. The most conservative member of the court, Associate Justice William Rehnquist, was appointed to replace retiring Chief Justice Warren Burger.

In Reagan's second term, Congress demanded a more active environmental policy. On October 17, 1986, a bill was signed into law that extended the Superfund hazardous waste cleanup program. Still, Reagan vetoed the reauthorization of the Clean Water Act, proclaiming that the $18 billion act was too expensive. In early 1987, following the 1986 midterm elections, Congress overrode Reagan's veto of the Water Quality Control Act, which was almost identical to the Clean Water Act.

IMMIGRATION REFORM AND CONTROL ACT OF 1986

Following more than five years of negotiations, during which a number of bills were proposed and failed, President Reagan signed a comprehensive immigration act on November 6, 1986. Named the Simpson-Mazzoli Bill after sponsors Senator Alan K. Simpson of Wyoming and Congressman Romano L. Mazzoli of Kentucky, the Immigration Reform and Control Act of 1986 increased the penalty for smuggling aliens into the country, and for the first time in history, made it a federal crime to hire aliens with the knowledge that they were in the country illegally. Fines ranged from $250 to $10,000 for each alien, as well as six months in prison in extreme cases. Although the bill became law in November 1986, the penalties did not apply until May 1988.

The act was meant to quell the rising number of illegal immigrants in the United States. Illegal aliens who could prove that they had arrived in the country after January 1, 1982, were automatically granted legal status. In addition, the bill included a provision that allowed 350,000 foreigners to be deemed temporary residents providing that they could prove they had worked in agriculture for at least 90 days between May 1985 and May 1986. This provision allowed western farmers who often hired illegal aliens to continue to employ an important pool of workers.

THE SPACE SHUTTLE *CHALLENGER*

On January 28, 1986, the U.S. space program suffered the worst accident in its history when the space shuttle

Associate Justice William Rehnquist was appointed chief justice upon the retirement of Warren Burger. *(Library of Congress)*

The crew of the space shuttle *Challenger* is pictured. In the first row from left to right are Michael J. Smith, Francis R. "Dick" Scobee, and Ronald E. McNair. In the second row from left to right are Ellison S. Onizuka, Sharon "Christa" McAuliffe, Gregory B. Jarvis, and Judith Resnick. *(NASA)*

Challenger exploded just over 73 seconds after liftoff from Florida's Cape Canaveral. The entire crew perished in the explosion, which was viewed by millions worldwide live on television. Onboard were Commander Francis R. "Dick" Scobee; Pilot Michael J. Smith; mission specialists Judith A. Resnik, Ronald E. McNair and Ellison S. Onizuka; Hughes Aircraft Corporation employee Gregory B. Jarvis; and high school teacher Sharon "Christa" McAuliffe.

The launch had originally been scheduled for January 22 but was delayed due to bad weather conditions. The president appointed an independent 13-member commission that included former astronaut Neil Armstrong and Nobel prize–winning physicist Richard P. Feynman and was chaired by former secretary of state William P. Rogers to investigate.

The Rogers Commission issued its report on June 6, 1986, which explained that the explosion was caused by the failure of rubber O-rings, which sealed the joints

THE FIRST TEACHER IN SPACE

The *Challenger* carried a crew of seven, including Christa McAuliffe, a high school teacher, when it exploded on January 28, 1986. More than 11,000 educators had applied for the opportunity to be the first teacher in space. Upon being selected to participate in the NASA Teacher in Space Program, the married mother of two took a leave of absence from teaching and trained for a year with NASA. She planned to teach two lessons from space and to keep a video journal of her experiences. In addition, her proposal to NASA included a three-part journaling project, in which she would detail her experiences, thoughts, and feelings during training, throughout the mission, and upon her return to Earth.

between sections of the solid rocket boosters and expanded as temperatures increased during the launch. In this case, the O-rings failed to expand, allowing hot gases to leak, which in turn ignited the main liquid fuel tank.

A freak cold spell in Florida was partly to blame for the O-ring failure. At least two engineers from Morton Thiokol, Inc., the company that manufactured the boosters, had voiced concern that at 36°F the climate was too cold for the launch. The engineers apparently had also repeatedly advised senior management that the O-rings were problematic. Thiokol and NASA spoke prior to the launch, and NASA deferred to Thiokol's decision. Unwilling to risk losing NASA's business, Thiokol recommended that the launch continue as planned.

The conclusion of Reagan's touching tribute to the *Challenger* crew became, perhaps, one of his best known quotes: "We will never forget them, nor the last time we saw them this morning as they prepared for their journey and waved good-bye and 'slipped the surly bonds of earth' to touch the face of God." On March 9, 1986, the U.S. Navy found the bodies of all seven astronauts inside the intact crew compartment.

THE IRAN-CONTRA SCANDAL BECOMES PUBLIC

By spring 1985, additional parties expressed interest in supporting the Contras. Oliver North dispatched John Singlaub, a retired army major general, to meet with

HAWK missiles like those depicted here were some of the illegal arms shipped to Iran as part of a plan to exchange arms for American hostages. *(DOD Defense Visual Information Center)*

officials from South Korea who knew outside support would be essential, because Congress appeared unwilling to lend more support to the Contras. This was clear when Congress denied an additional $14 million in aid to the Contras in March 1985. On May 1, 1985, Reagan denounced the Sandinsta government and ordered a trade embargo on Nicaragua.

In August, however, Congress approved $27 million in humanitarian aid for the Contras provided that the State Department rather than the CIA administer the funding. The Nicaraguan Humanitarian Assistance Office (NHAO) was also established within the State Department.

Despite the Congressional mandate barring CIA involvement, the agency used the NHAO in its dealings with the Contras. In addition, personnel that had been working covertly with North and retired army general Richard Secord, North's arms dealer, were placed within the office. Secord illegally sold arms to Iran so that Iran would release hostages held by anti-American forces, the money raised by arms sales went to support the Contras. When Congress inquired about North's activities, National Security Advisor Bud McFarlane and North decided to lie about the latter's activities.

The first illegal arms shipment to Iran arrived on August 20, 1985, when 2,004 TOW antitank and 18 HAWK antiaircraft missiles, in addition to 240 spare HAWK parts, were delivered to Teheran. On its part, Iran arranged the release of three U.S. hostages in Lebanon. With Reagan's consent, Israel acted as a conduit for the arms transfers in 1985.

In June 1986, the House approved an additional $100 million humanitarian and economic aid to the Contras. Within days, the International Court of Justice ruled that such aid was illegal and ordered payment of reparations, a mandate that the United States ignored.

TERROR AT SEA

On October 7, 1985, terrorists from the Palestine Liberation Front seized the Italian cruise ship *Achille Lauro as* it traveled in the Mediterranean near Egypt. Demanding the release of 50 Palestinian prisoners by Israel, they killed 69-year old American passenger Leon Klinghoffer, who was confined to a wheelchair, and threw his body overboard.

American support of the Contras was revealed on October 5, 1986, when the Sandinistas shot down a U.S. cargo plane filled with weapons and other supplies. While held captive, the pilot and sole survivor of the three crew members, Eugene Hasenfus, confessed that he had been hired by the CIA to deliver the cargo to the Contras. On November 3, the Lebanese magazine *Ash-Shiraa* ran a story exposing the arms for hostages program.

Although Reagan initially denied Hasenfus's claim, on November 13, 1986, Congressional leaders were informed that the United States had supplied Iran with defense weapons and spare parts. Oliver North and his secretary, Fawn Hall, meanwhile, began to shred evidence of the sale of arms for hostages and the funneling of funds to the Contras. Exactly six days later, Reagan asked Attorney General Edwin Meese to investigate the sale of missiles to Iraq, and on November 23, Meese acknowledged the diversion of funds to the Contras.

On November 25, the Reagan administration acknowledged that anywhere between $10 and $30 million of the funds obtained through arms sales to Iran

Attorney General Edwin Meese (center) is pictured with Secretary of the Treasury James Baker III (left) and Michael Deaver (right), Reagan's aide. *(Ronald Reagan Library)*

At the request of German chancellor Helmut Kohl, President Reagan attended a wreath-laying ceremony at a military cemetery in Bitburg, West Germany, on May 5, 1985. The visit provoked protest when it was discovered that 49 Nazis and members of Adolf Hitler's military police were included among the 2,000 soldiers buried at the cemetery.

had been used to fund military aid to the Contras. On December 1, 1986, Reagan appointed a commission to investigate the Iran-Contra affair. The Tower Commission included former senator John Tower, former Secretary of State Edmund Muskie, and former national security advisor Brent Scowcroft.

STRAINED RELATIONS WITH LIBYA

In January 1986, the United States declared that the government of Libya, led by General Muammar al-Qadhafi, had sponsored terrorist acts and responded by imposing economic sanctions on the country. In March of that year, Libya fired antiaircraft missiles at U.S. military planes that were conducting exercises in the Gulf of Syria and had strayed over an unofficial boundary that Libya had named the "Line of Death." The United States retaliated by attacking Libyan missile sites and ships, and one month later, blamed Libya for the death of two American servicemen in the explosion of a Berlin nightclub.

On April 14–15, bombing raids were conducted on Qadhafi's home in Tripoli and other strategic targets in Libya. The United States lost one plane and its crew in the raids. Great Britain alone supported America's cause, allowing the U.S. Air Force to dispatch its planes from their bases. Other NATO allies rejected America's request to fly over their airspace.

THE PHILIPPINES

In February 1985, Ferdinand Marcos, the president of the Philippines, resigned his office and fled to the United States, where he received safe haven. Almost two years earlier, his rival, Benigno Aquino, had been killed by Marcos's security guards at the airport when he returned from a self-imposed exile. Throughout 1984, Filipinos protested Marcos's regime. The United

States continued to support him because the administration feared losing access to the air force and navy bases in the Philippines.

As 1984 began to draw to a close, Aquino's widow, Corazon, announced that she would run for president. On election day, however, Marcos named himself the winner, resulting in more protests. Once military leaders joined the protests, the Reagan administration condemned Marcos as well, and he fled the country. The United States threw its support behind Aquino, putting together emergency funding for the poverty-stricken country. Still, in the late 1980s, when Aquino accused Marcos of stealing from his constituency, the United States refused to deport him.

GLASNOST AND PERESTROIKA

Konstantin Chernenko, general secretary of the Central Committee of the Communist Party, died on March 11, 1985. The following day, 54-year old Mikhail Gorbachev assumed leadership of the party. With his candid declaration that there were problems with communism, Gorbachev opened doors for relations with the United States. Far younger than the general secretaries who immediately preceded him, Gorbachev infused the party with new blood and more progressive ideas and goals. *Glasnost,* or openness in communication and government decisions, and *perestroika,* referring to the political reform and economic reconstruction of the USSR, became household words in the United States. Gorbachev encouraged not only the development of small businesses, including craftsmen, among his own countrymen but also welcomed enterprises by foreign companies into the USSR.

In November 1985, Reagan and Gorbachev met for the first time in Geneva, Switzerland, marking the first such meeting between the two nation's leaders in six years. To celebrate, televised messages from Reagan and

President Reagan, seen here with General Matthew Ridgeway, caused an uproar by attending a wreath-laying ceremony at Bitburg Cemetery in West Germany where Nazis and members of Adolf Hitler's military police are buried. *(Ronald Reagan Library)*

Soviet general secretary Mikhail Gorbachev and President Reagan met for the first time in Geneva, Switzerland, in November 1985. *(Ronald Reagan Library)*

Gorbachev were broadcast in each other's countries on New Year's Day 1986. Another summit followed in Reykjavik, Iceland, in October 1986. In Reykjavik, Reagan and Gorbachev reached an agreement regarding strategic and medium-range nuclear missiles and nuclear testing, among other things. The Reagan administration's policy toward SDI, however, resulted in a breakdown in the summit. The Soviets feared that the development of a defensive shield of such magnitude could encourage the use of offensive weapons. They were also concerned about the system's reliance on highly sensitive, as of yet undeveloped technology that might malfunction.

"Our duty to all human kind is to offer it a safe prospect of peace, a prospect of entering the third millennium without fear."

—General Secretary Mikhail Gorbachev, January 1, 1986, during a televised address to the United States

ROCK 'N' ROLL FOR A CAUSE

Irishman Bob Geldof, the lead singer of the Boomtown Rats and one of the masterminds behind the all-star single "Do They Know It's Christmas?," which raised funds for famine relief in Africa, planned two more similar concerts. Called Live-Aid, the star-studded events took place simultaneously on July 13, 1985, at Wembley Stadium in London, and JFK Stadium in Philadelphia, and were aired live on television to almost 2 billion viewers worldwide. The 16-hour live music program saw performances by Queen, Tina Turner, Mick Jagger, David Bowie, U2, Dire

Straits, Wham, the Beach Boys, Paul Simon, Duran Duran, Sting, Run DMC, and Phil Collins, who famously performed at Wembley, hopped on the Concord, flew to the United States, and then performed at the JFK Stadium. Almost $140 million was raised for famine relief.

Michael Jackson and Lionel Richie joined forces with producer Quincy Jones and a bevy of stars to record another single for African famine relief entitled "We Are the World." Bruce Springsteen, Billy Joel, Cyndi Lauper, Diana Ross, Stevie Wonder, Bob Dylan, and many others performed the song, which was released in March 1985 and raised $50 million. The song also won Record of the Year and Song of the Year at the 1985 Grammy awards.

On September 22, 1985, musical performers united for another cause: Farm Aid. Co-founders Willie Nelson, John Mellencamp, and Neil Young organized this benefit for America's farmers, raising $10 million. Farm Aid concerts have since become an annual event, with the funds raised being used for emergency situations often caused by natural disasters, hotlines for farmers struggling with emotional and financial issues, legal support for farmers and farming advocates, education programs for farmers regarding financial and policy issues, and outreach and development supporting family farm agriculture.

On May 25, 1986, more than 5 million Americans participated in Hands Across America, a fundraising event for homelessness and hunger. Participants paid $10 each, and the money was donated to local shelters.

A star-studded concert held simultaneously in Philadelphia and London, Live-Aid was a benefit for Ethopian famine relief. *(Paul Natkin/Photo Reserve)*

GAMES: BOARD AND VIDEO

The game Pictionary, in which players draw a picture representing a phrase or a word, and their teammates have to guess it, was introduced in Seattle in 1985. By 1987, sales hit the $3 million mark. Following the path paved by Atari, Nintendo video game systems, which debuted in 1985, topped $830 million in sales by 1987. By the end of the decade, sales exceeded $2 billion.

"Graffiti art is an instant gesture, like calligraphy. And because I'm capturing that instant, I do not believe in mistakes."

—Artist Keith Haring in *ARTNews*, November 1985

A family enjoys a video game on the Atari system. Atari took the country by storm, paving the way for the acceptance of the more complex and expensive Atari systems that dominated the market into the late 1990s. *(Atari)*

"There has been progress, but we do not want apartheid ameliorated or improved. We do not want apartheid made comfortable. We want it dismantled."

—Desmond Tutu, Anglican archibishop-elect of Cape Town, South Africa

On January 23, 1986, the Rock and Roll Hall of Fame inducted its first honorees, including Chuck Berry, Ray Charles, Fats Domino, James Brown, the Everly Brothers, Jerry Lee Lewis, Buddy Holly, and Elvis Presley.

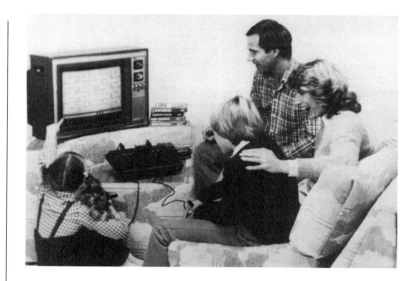

A song by the same name was played at 3:00 P.M. (Eastern time) nationwide.

For another cause, Steven Van Zandt, guitarist for Bruce Springsteen's E Street band, coordinated Artists United Against Apartheid. An all-star group including Miles Davis, Run-DMC, Lou Reed, Bob Dylan, Bonnie Raitt, and others cut the single "Sun City," which admonished performers not to play in the South African resort Sun City as a protest against apartheid. Singer/songwriter Paul Simon, meanwhile, stirred up controversy by recording part of his 1986 release *Graceland* in South Africa, in which South African performers such as Ladysmith Black Mambazo were featured.

OTHER MUSIC

Rap music evolved in the South Bronx in the late 1970s and early 1980s, but it was not until Run DMC remade the Aerosmith song "Walk This Way" that the genre found its way into the general population. The song hit No.4 on the charts and introduced mainstream America to a new genre of music. Rap captured the feelings of disenfranchised black youth, much like heavy metal did for white male teens.

WASHINGTON WIVES TAKE ON ROCK 'N' ROLL

Concerned that rock 'n' roll lyrics were too violent and overtly sexual, Tipper Gore, the wife of Senator Al Gore, and other Washington wives founded the Parent's Music Resource Center (PMRC). Along with the National PTA, the PMRC worked to establish a ratings system for records to be used by the National Recording Industry Association of America. Although the association refused to implement a ratings system, they did advocate Explicit Lyrics—Parental Advisory labels for some recordings. Frank Zappa, John Denver, and Dee Snyder (of Twisted Sister) all testified before Congress on behalf of artists' rights.

Tipper Gore, wife of Senator Al Gore, testified on behalf of the Parent's Music Resource Center (PMRC). *(AP/Wide World Photos)*

"No one has forced Mrs. Baker or Mrs. Gore to bring Prince or Sheena Easton into their homes.... Ladies, how dare you?"

—Frank Zappa, statement to Congress, September 19, 1985

Bands like Def Leppard, Quiet Riot, Van Halen, and AC/DC gave teenage boys an outlet to vent their feelings. Hard rock/heavy metal was loud, and these bands lived the rock star life to the hilt. These bands provided an alternative to the pop that was on the radio. For teenage boys, as well as some teenage girls, hard rock was the antidote to softer hits by the Bangles, Starship, and Billy Ocean.

TELEVISION

In December 1985, General Electric (GE) paid $6.3 billion to acquire Radio Corporation of America (RCA) and the National Broadcasting Company (NBC). GE's acquisition of NBC marked the third major change in the big three network ownership in 1985. Capital City Communications bought the American Broadcasting Company (ABC) in March, and Laurence Tisch and the Loews Corporation acquired the Central Broadcasting

Among the most popular album releases of 1986 were *So* by Peter Gabriel, *Graceland* by Paul Simon, and Police front man Sting's first solo effort, *The Dream of the Blue Turtles.* (Michele L. Camardella)

In April, the public met a change in Coca-Cola's formula with hostility. The company renamed their old formula "Classic Coke" and resumed its production.

System (CBS) in October. In addition, the FOX Broadcasting Company was founded as the fourth television network.

In cable news, the Home Shopping Network (HSN) was available nationally and boasted over 75,000 regular customers by 1985. HSN had been founded in Florida as a radio program and moved to local cable in the 1970s, providing another opportunity to shop from home. Suddenly, in 1986, HSN faced competition from 17 other stations, including Quality, Value, Convenience (QVC) that ultimately became HSN's major rival.

The television show *Moonlighting* debuted in 1985, starring Cybill Shepherd as a model turned private investigator who runs an agency with a wise-cracking detective played by newcomer Bruce Willis. Fashioned after the screwball romantic comedies of the 1930s, the show experimented with techniques such as addressing the audience directly. In 1986, *The Oprah Winfrey Show* went into syndication on 138 stations. The next year the show received three Emmy awards and expanded to 180 stations.

FILM

The Brat Pack phenomenon continued in 1985 and 1986, with more movies being released featuring young actors and geared toward teenagers. *The Breakfast Club,* released in 1985, challenged the stereotypes into which teens are relegated, as did *Pretty in Pink* (1986), both starring Molly Ringwald. The young 20-somethings in *St. Elmo's Fire* had trouble leaving their college days behind and taking adulthood seriously. Judd Nelson, Rob Lowe, Andrew McCarthy, Ally Sheedy, Anthony Michael Hall, and other actors, including Demi Moore, Sean Penn, and Charlie Sheen were considered Brat Packers. Although not necessarily considered part of the pack, Matthew Broderick joined the teen movie revolution with *Ferris Bueller's Day Off* (1986), starring as a fun-loving high school senior who skips school for the day and takes his friends on an adventure through Chicago.

In addition, *Krush Groove,* the first film to feature rap, was released in 1985. On the other end of the spectrum, David Lynch's avant garde film *Blue Velvet* starred Dennis Hopper and Isabella Rosellini. Spike Lee made his directorial debut with *She's Gotta Have It. Aliens* featured Sigourney Weaver as a female action hero fighting a monster in space.

SCIENCE AND TECHNOLOGY

On September 1, 1985, a French-American team led by Dr. Robert D. Ballard spotted the wreckage of the *Titanic*—the luxury liner that had sailed from Queenstown, County Cork, on April, 11, 1912, and sank three days later after colliding with an iceberg—1,000 miles due east of Boston, Massachusetts. Almost one year later, on July 26, 1986, Ballard returned to explore the wreckage, and left a plaque in memory of those who perished and to commemorate the Titanic Historical Society.

According to the British Antarctic Survey, a hole (or extreme thinning) in the ozone layer was discovered to have expanded above Antarctica in 1985. The ozone layer, which protects the Earth from the ultraviolet rays of the sun, was also reported to be thinning in other areas of the globe. Chemicals commonly used in a variety of everyday objects, such as air conditioners, aerosol cans, refrigerators, insulation, and cleaning solutions contained harmful, ozone-depleting substances that led to the thinning. A movement was soon formed to reduce the use of such chemicals, known as chlorofluorocarbons (CFCs).

THE AIDS EPIDEMIC ESCALATES

AIDS victims continued to battle discrimination in many arenas, including the workplace. In fact, it was

> The graphite core of a reactor at the Chernobyl nuclear power plant near Kiev in the Ukraine caught fire on April 28, 1986, resulting in extremely high levels of radiation in the surrounding area. In the weeks following the accident, more than 30 plant workers and firefighters died, and tens of thousands fell ill.

A fire in a reactor at the Chernobyl nuclear power plant near Kiev released high levels or radiation into the area, resulting in deaths and illness. *(AP/Wide World Photos)*

Protesters took to the streets to demand more funding for AIDS research. *(Corbis)*

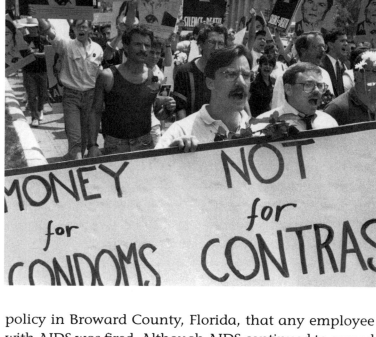

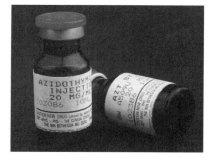

Clinical trials of a new drug, azidothymidine (AZT), gave AIDS victims new hope. *(NIH)*

policy in Broward County, Florida, that any employee with AIDS was fired. Although AIDS continued to spread internationally, it was still viewed largely as a disease affecting gay American men. In 1985, 67 percent of all newly reported AIDS cases resulted from male homosexual contact, 17 percent from IV drug users, 14 percent from other (blood transfusions, those who claimed none of the other reasons), and 2 percent from heterosexual contact. Almost two-thirds of the 4,000 AIDS-related deaths reported by 1985 were people under the age of 40.

The revelation that movie star Rock Hudson had contracted AIDS shocked many Americans, including the president. In fact, Reagan's get-well call to his old Hollywood friend marked the first real interest he showed regarding the disease. On October 5, 1985, the day Hudson died, the House of Representatives doubled the funds for AIDS research to $189 million. The Senate Appropriations Committee followed suit, raising AIDS funding to a total of $221 million. In fall 1986, clinical trials proved the drug azidothymidine (AZT) slowed the progress of the AIDS virus. Still, the disease killed in devastating numbers. By the end of 1986, 38,401 cases of AIDS had been reported in 85 countries worldwide. The United States accounted for 31,741 of these cases.

SPORTS

Martina Navratilova won her 100th tennis match in January 1985. That same month, well known running back and actor O. J. Simpson was elected to the Football Hall of Fame. On July 27, 1986, Greg LeMond won the Tour de France cycling race, becoming the first American to do so. Mike Tyson, 21, became the youngest heavyweight boxing champion by defeating Trevor Berbick, the World Boxing Council champ. In April 1986, Jack Nicklaus won a record-setting sixth Masters. He also became the oldest player to win this golf competition.

The 1986 World Series had New York Mets and Boston Red Sox fans on the edge of their seats. The tenth inning of game six proved to be one of the most

The New York Mets won the 1986 World Series against the Boston Red Sox. *(National Baseball Hall of Fame Library and Museum)*

riveting in baseball history. The Red Sox managed to take the lead in game six and were just one out away from winning the Series when the Mets hit two singles in a row. With just one strike keeping the Red Sox from the title, the Mets hit another single. Then their outfielder, Mookie Wilson, hit a ground ball toward first base following a full count. When the ball got away from the Red Sox first baseman Bill Buckner, Mets player Ray Knight, who was waiting on third, ran home, securing a game six victory for the Mets. The Mets won game seven, taking the 1986 series, and giving credence to the curse of the Bambino, which attributed the Red Sox World Series losing streak to the sale of Babe Ruth to the Yankees in 1920.

CHAPTER 5

THE ECONOMY TAKES A DIVE, 1987

John Tower (left), President Reagan, and Edmund Muskie review the Tower Commission Report about the Iran-Contra affair. *(Ronald Reagan Library)*

THE ECONOMY APPEARED STRONG IN 1987. The Dow Jones Industrial Average—the most widely used indicator of the overall condition of the stock market, a price-weighted average of 30 actively traded blue chip stocks, primarily industrials—closed above 2,700 points for the first time in August. By October, however, the scenario had changed. On October 19, 1987, the stock market fell 508 points in one day, setting a new record. Just six months later, the economy seemed to have rebounded again, with unemployment at 5.6 percent, the lowest in a decade. Unfortunately, not every part of the economy rebounded. Family farms continued to suffer, the market for exports was not increasing, and the U.S. dollar declined in value compared to other international monies.

"A few months ago I told the American people I did not trade arms for hostages. My heart and best intentions still tell me that's true, but the facts and the evidence tell me it is not. . . . as president, I cannot escape responsibility."

—President Ronald Reagan, March 4, 1987, regarding the Iran-Contra scandal

Under Reagan's leadership between 1982 and 1987, the average annual deficit was more than $180 billion, resulting in a total deficit during this period of more than $1.1 trillion. In order to handle this debt, hundreds of billions of dollars were borrowed from other nations, and the United States—which had historically been one of the largest lender nations in the world—became one of the world's largest debtor nations. When Reagan assumed office in 1981, the national debt was $914 billion and annual interest totaled $71 billion. When he left office in January 1989, the debt was $2.6 trillion and interest payments totaled $152 billion.

Reagan's luck with appointments to the Supreme Court ran out in fall 1987, when he nominated Appellate Judge Robert Bork to the Court. Bork was considered to have extreme views regarding the First Amendment, and the Senate rejected his nomination. Reagan's second candidate, Donald Ginsburg, withdrew when it was discovered that he had smoked marijuana, not only while a student at Harvard but also while teaching at Harvard Law School.

THE IRAN-CONTRA SCANDAL

The Tower Commission report regarding the Iran-Contra situation was released on February 27, 1987. While the report did not accuse Reagan of criminal misdoing or personally implicate him in the scandal, the commission did hold the president ultimately responsible for the turn of events. White House chief of staff Donald Regan resigned the day after the commission issued its report. On May 4, 1987, the president claimed full responsibility for the scandal in a television address to the American public.

On May 5, 1987, congressional hearings began. In total, 28 witnesses would testify for approximately 250 hours over a period of 11 weeks. The investigation

U.S. Marine lieutenant colonel Oliver North spent six days under oath testifying about the arms for hostages scandal. *(AP/Wide World Photos)*

revealed that U.S. Marine lieutenant colonel Oliver North had coordinated efforts to sell arms to Iran and used the proceeds to aid the Contras, running the operation out of an office in the basement of the White House. While under oath during six days of hearings in July 1987, Colonel North implicated the attorney general, and the president as well as CIA director William Casey, who had died in May of that year. That same month, the former chief of the National Security Council, Rear Admiral John M. Poindexter, testified that he had authorized monies from the sale of arms to Iran to be diverted to the Contras. In March 1988, North was indicted on 16 counts. McFarlane, meanwhile, pleaded guilty to withholding information from Congress.

Some other areas of Central America remained hotbeds of activity as well. The Reagan administration became involved with Panama when drug trafficking, repression, and corruption existing under General Manuel Antonio Noriega was disclosed. Allegedly, because Noriega had aided the Contras and was a CIA informant, the U.S. government had ignored concerns regarding Noriega's rule. Eventually, the United States responded to Panamanian opposition against Noriega and imposed economic sanctions and increased military pressure in an attempt to force him out. In February of the following year, the United States failed in its efforts to extradite Noriega, who had been indicted for drug trafficking and racketeering charges in Florida.

In March 1987, the United States offered its protection to Kuwaiti tankers in the Persian Gulf, where attacks from Iran remained a threat. On May 17, 1987, 37 sailors aboard the U.S. Navy frigate *Stark* were killed by an accidental Iraqi missile attack. *(DOD Defense Visual Information Center)*

TELEVISION'S NEW ROLE

Throughout the 1980s, televangelists had gained popularity, attracting millions of followers. The Moral Majority, founded by the Reverend Jerry Falwell in 1979, had a membership of nearly 2 million by the mid-1980s, and by 1985, his television show had an audience numbering approximately 5 million.

THE VIGILANTE

On June 16, 1987, a New York State Supreme Court jury, composed of 10 white and two black jurors, acquitted Bernhard Goetz of 12 of the 13 charges brought against him. Goetz shot four black youths on a New York City subway in December 1984. Because the youths had asked him for $5, Goetz determined that they intended to mug him and claimed to have shot them in self-defense. In October 1987, he was fined $5,000 and received a six-month jail sentence.

A TREATY WITH THE USSR

On December 8, 1987, Reagan and Gorbachev met at the White House to sign the Intermediate-Range Nuclear Forces (INF) Treaty, agreeing to destroy more than 850 American nuclear missiles in Europe and more than 1,800 Soviet missiles in Europe within three years. With this historic treaty, the two superpowers agreed to reduce nuclear weapons for the first time.

Soviet General Secretary Gorbachev and President Reagan made history by signing the Intermediate-Range Nuclear Forces (INF) Treaty, which curtailed U.S. and Soviet nuclear weapons. *(Ronald Reagan Library)*

In March 1987, Oral Roberts proclaimed that if he failed to raise $8 million by the end of the month, God might call him home (meaning he might die). His viewers responded, and Roberts was able to save his ministry, which included a medical school and Oral Roberts University. But two years later, Roberts closed the medical school and a hospital, and sold his home to finance debt that had been accumulated by his university.

In June 1987, however, scandals marred the reputation of prominent televangelists. Jim and Tammy Faye Bakker of Praise the Lord, also known as People That Love, (PTL) ministries, and Jimmy Swaggart, religious leaders and ministers who lead their congregations via television shows, were involved in a battle for control of Heritage USA, a Gospel-themed amusement park and complex in Fort Mills, South Carolina.

Heritage USA included a mall, a hotel tower, television studios, a farm, an adoption agency, a prison outreach initiative, a drug rehabilitation facility, retirement housing, a dinner theater, time-shares, and condominiums. The death knell sounded for Bakker's empire on March 19, 1987, when he admitted that he had engaged in illicit actions with Jessica Hahn, a church secretary in Long Island, New York, and paid her $265,000 in ministry funds as hush money. Bakker stepped down as leader of the PTL.

Jim and Tammy Faye Bakker were among the televangelists who were implicated in scandals in the late 1980s. *(AP/Wide World Photos)*

Upon Bakker's resignation, Jerry Falwell temporarily assumed leadership of the multimillion dollar empire and uncovered financial abuses by the Bakkers and their staff. Through various outlets, including programs aired on 140 television stations and a Lifetime Partners plan at the Heritage Towers Hotel, the PTL was generating multimillion dollar revenues each month. The Bakkers had paid themselves salaries and perks totaling almost $5 million over the course of three and a half years. When Falwell assumed control of the empire, he discovered that the organization had more than 45 separate checking accounts and was $72 million in debt. On June 1, 1987, the U.S. Justice Department announced an inquiry into Heritage USA, including allegations of tax evasion, mail fraud, and tax-exempt status issues. On October 5, 1989, after 10 hours of deliberation, a jury found Bakker guilty of fraud. He was sentenced to 45 years in prison and fined $500,000.

Cable television continued to expand in the late 1980s, boasting an increase of 2 million households from 1986 to 1987 to reach a total of 43.2 million households. Cable channels were able to offer unedited, commercial free movies, as well as content that was more racy than that allowed on network television. Cable and video casette recorders (VCRs) changed the way people viewed films, and the way that a film earned money. By 1987, more revenue was derived from videotape rentals of movies and their cable broadcasts

"Those of us who do have a religion are sick of being saps for money-grubbing preachers and priests."

—U.S. District Judge Robert Potter at the sentencing of televangelist Jim Bakker, October 5, 1989

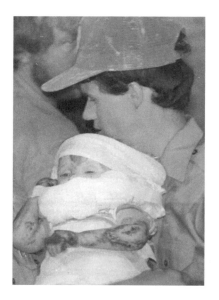

Eighteen-month old Jessica McClure was rescued 58 hours after falling 22 feet down an abandoned well in Midland, Texas. *(AP/Wide World Photos)*

Jon Bon Jovi's band, Bon Jovi, gained popularity with their album *Slippery When Wet.* *(Paul Natkin/Photo Reserve)*

than from ticket sales. In addition, network television suffered from the expansion of VCRs, which by 1988 were in 58 percent of American homes.

The ensemble show *thirtysomething* debuted in 1987, garnering both acclaim and disdain from critics and the public. While many felt that the show realistically depicted the everyday lives of those in their thirties, others complained that the show was about yuppies who just whined too much. In the sitcom world, *Roseanne* debuted, offering realistic insight into the lives of America's working class families. *The Wonder Years* also debuted, featuring a grown man's memories of his childhood in the 1960s.

Perhaps the most riveting television of 1987, however, was the saga of Jessica McClure or "Baby Jessica." The 18-month old toddler had fallen 22 feet down an abandoned well that measured only eight inches wide in Midland, Texas. America watched for 58 hours as workers struggled to free the child, who sang to herself to pass the time until she was rescued.

MUSIC

Rap music continued to grow in popularity in the late 1980s. The Beastie Boys hit the jackpot with "(You Gotta) Fight for the Right (to Party)" from *Licensed to Ill.* Michael Jackson's younger sister, Janet, emerged as an independent young woman with the album *Control.* Hard rockers Bon Jovi led the so-called hair band invasion with guitar-driven rock and roll that was radio-friendly with their album *Slippery When Wet.* Def Leppard joined them on the charts with *Hysteria.* Pop singer George Michael, meanwhile, went solo with *Faith,* leaving his band Wham! behind. But the year belonged to the socially conscious Irish band U2, whose megahit album *The Joshua Tree* spawned the hit singles "With or Without You," "Where the Streets Have No Name," and "I Still Haven't Found What I'm Looking For."

FILM

During the latter half of the 1980s, many films dealt with the Vietnam War and its effect on the soldiers who fought it. Although *Platoon* and *Heartbreak Ridge* began the trend in 1986, they were quickly followed in 1987 by *Full Metal Jacket, Hamburger Hill, Gardens of Stone,* and *Good Morning, Vietnam.*

In *Fatal Attraction,* Glenn Close played Alex Forrest, a single woman who has a one-night stand with a married man and then becomes dangerously obsessed with him. Jennifer Grey played an idealistic teenager in the 1960s who falls in love with a dance instructor from the streets (Patrick Swayze) at a Catskills resort in *Dirty Dancing.* As Gordon Gekko in *Wall Street,* Michael Douglas epitomized the greed of 1980s culture—and ultimately won the Oscar for Best Actor. Cher, meanwhile, won an Oscar for her performance in *Moonstruck.*

SPORTS

In response to a 24-day NFL players' strike in 1987, management cancelled the first games of the season. Games resumed with teams composed of replacement players and some NFL players who did not participate in the strike. The Los Angeles Lakers defeated the Boston Celtics to clinch the NBA championship. Ron Hextall of the Philadelphia Flyers became the first goalie to shoot and score a goal in NHL history.

In baseball, the Minnesota Twins and the St. Louis Cardinals played the first indoor World Series. The Twins won the series four games to three in a surprise victory. Prior to the game, the Twins had 150-1 odds of winning. The love/hate relationship between New York Yankees owner George Steinbrenner and manager Billy

> *"The point is, ladies and gentlemen, that greed—for lack of a better word—is good."*
>
> —Michael Douglas as Gordon Gekko in Oliver Stone's film *Wall Street,* 1987

In 1987, Aretha Franklin became the first woman to be inducted to the Rock and Roll Hall of Fame.

Home to the Minnesota Twins, the Metrodome, with its air-supported roof, revolutionized indoor stadium construction when it opened in Minneapolis in 1982 and hosted the first indoor World Series in 1987. *(National Baseball Hall of Fame Library and Museum)*

THE SURROGATE MOM DEBATE

Surrogate motherhood took center stage when Mary Beth Whitehead of Brick Town, New Jersey, decided that she wanted to keep the child that she had contractually agreed to carry for William and Elizabeth Stern. Whitehead had been inseminated with Stern's sperm. She signed a $10,000 contract and agreed to cede all parental rights upon delivery. When the child was born, however, Whitehead's maternal instincts overwhelmed her. Although the Sterns were granted custody of the child, who was deemed Baby M, Whitehead and her husband took the baby to Florida, where they remained for 87 days until a private investigator regained Baby M for the Sterns. A seven-week trial ensued, marking the first time a surrogacy agreement went to court. On March 31, 1987, the Sterns won custody of Baby M, and Whitehead was denied all parental rights.

Martin continued when Steinbrenner hired Martin for the fifth time in October 1987; he would fire Martin as manager in June 1988.

International boxing underwent a makeover in 1987 when new weight classes were introduced by the World Boxing Council (WBC). In other boxing news, Mike Tyson became the first undisputed heavyweight champion since Muhammad Ali. The same year, middleweight Sugar Ray Leonard made a comeback at age 30, defeating opponent Marvin Hagler despite spending three years out of the ring. Following a 10-year retirement, former heavyweight champion George Foreman returned to the ring and defeated Steve Zouski.

SCIENCE AND TECHNOLOGY

In September 1987, lovastatin (Mevacor), a drug that lowered cholesterol, was approved by the Food and Drug Administration (FDA). The FDA also approved tissue plasminogen activator (TPA; Activase) a new substance that dissolved blood clots, and an existing one, streptokinase (Streptase) for the emergency treatment of heart attack victims. The antidepressant Prozac debuted in the United States on December 29, 1987.

Scientists testified about ozone depletion before Congress, and a Montreal summit set new standards regarding chlorofluorocarbon aerosol propellants (CFCs) in an effort to reduce their use. The scientific world also pondered the greenhouse effect, the theory proposing that increases in carbon dioxide led to the Earth's warming. This theory took the spotlight when an iceberg broke away from the Ross Ice Shelf in Antarctica because of the unusually warm conditions resulting from El Niño, a disruption of the ocean-atmosphere system in the tropical Pacific having important consequences for weather around the globe.

Evidence suggesting the existence of black holes in space was found, and scientists discovered a crater

JUST SAY NO TO SMOKING

With Surgeon General C. Everett Koop's support, antismoking groups worked diligently. Smoking was restricted or banned in various areas, including schools, public buildings, restaurants, and corporate offices by 40 states, along with hundreds of cities and towns. A new industry sprung up as smokers spent $100 million on programs, clinics, and medications to help them kick the habit.

U.S. Surgeon General C. Everett Koop (right) embarked on an anti-smoking smoking campaign that found support from antismoking activist Patrick Reynolds (left), grandson of tobacco company founder R. J. Reynolds. *(TobaccoFree.org)*

On July 6, 1987, Martha Stewart, who built an empire based on cooking, crafts, and home decorating, signed on as the lifestyle spokesperson for the budget retailer K-Mart.

created by the impact of a meteor on the floor of the North Atlantic Ocean. In computers, IBM released their newest PC and operating system, the PS/2 and the OS/2.

THE AIDS EPIDEMIC

AIDS continued to take lives, crossing sexuality, race, creed, and nationality. By February 1987, almost 44,000 cases had been reported in 91 countries, including the first reported case in the Soviet Union. That same year in San Francisco, gay rights activist Cleve Jones made a quilt panel in memory of his friend and AIDS victim Marvin

Following gall bladder surgery, pop artist Andy Warhol died of a heart attack in February 1987.

President Reagan visited the National Institute of Health to announce the formation of a 13-member Commission on Human Immunodeficiency Virus Epidemic in July 1987. *(National Institutes of Health)*

CHILDREN LIVING IN POVERTY

According to the U.S. Bureau of the Census, in 1987, 13 million children under the age of 18 lived in poverty in the United States. Minorities seemed to be especially hard hit: 45.8 percent of black children and 39.8 percent of Hispanic children were poor. In addition, one of every five children lived in a female-headed household, and 54.7 percent of these children lived in poverty. Again, mainly minorities were affected: 68.3 percent of black children and 70.1 percent of Hispanic children in female-headed households were poor.

Feldman. The AIDS Memorial Quilt was created to celebrate and remember those who had succumbed to the disease. One year later, 80,000 victims had been immortalized in 42,000 quilt panels, each measuring three feet by six feet.

The AIDS Coalition to Unleash Power (ACT UP) was founded in spring 1987, dedicated to helping find a cure for the disease, increasing public education regarding AIDS, ending discrimination against AIDS victims, and making medical drugs available at more affordable prices. The group often used a symbolic pink triangle with the slogan "Silence = Death," which came to be associated with AIDS activism.

Throughout the first term of his presidency, Reagan made little mention of AIDS. In April 1987, however, while addressing the Philadelphia College of Physicians, he made his first major speech on the topic. He spoke on AIDS again on May 31, 1987, at a dinner for the American Foundation for AIDS Research (AmFar). His comments that focused largely on increasing volunteer work and mandatory testing provoked protest. The following day, protesters were arrested outside the White House, and Vice President Bush was booed while defending Reagan's comments at the opening of the Third Annual International Conference on AIDS in Washington, D.C. Exactly six years after the disease surfaced in America, the Reagan administration was finally speaking about the disease, but not everyone liked what they heard. As 1987 drew to a close, the number of AIDS cases totaled almost 72,000 internationally. More than 42,000 cases were reported in the United States alone.

CHAPTER 6

THE REAGAN ERA ENDS, 1988

AS REAGAN'S FINAL YEAR IN OFFICE and the 1988 presidential campaign began, domestic issues took center stage. From women's reproductive rights to punitive drug laws, the nation seemed to move in a more socially conservative direction. In 1988, family planning centers receiving federal funding were forbidden to discuss abortion with patients. That same year Randall Terry founded Operation Rescue, a group that blocked access to women's clinics where abortions were performed, and in *Bowen v. Kendrick* the Supreme Court supported a decision that denied federal funding to pro-choice programs.

Vice president George H. W. Bush and Democratic nominee Michael Dukakis, governor of Massachusetts, faced off in the 1988 presidential campaign. *(George Bush Presidential Library)*

The Omnibus Trade and Competitiveness Act of 1988 (OTC) included the Plant-Closing Bill, which required employers with more than 100 workers to provide 60 days notice of lay-offs or plant closings. Reagan opposed the Plant-Closing Bill, holding that such notice should be on a voluntary basis, and vetoed the OTC in May 1988. Eventually the OTC was separated into a trade bill, which Reagan signed into law, and the Plant-Closing Bill, which received more than a 2/3 vote in both the House and the Senate. Although Reagan did not veto the Plant-Closing Bill, he also did not sign it, instead letting it be approved by Congress without his support.

Congress continued to support Reagan's war on drugs, passing a $2.8 billion plan in its last act in 1988. The bill increased penalties for minor drug-related offenses, allocated more funds for drug education and treatment programs, and allowed for death penalty for drug-related murders. However, only $500 million of this plan could be spent in 1989 as a result of the balanced budget act.

"Where was George?"

—Delegates at the 1988 Democratic National Convention questioning where George H. W. Bush was during the Iran-Contra affair among other issues

PRESIDENTIAL CAMPAIGN AND ELECTION

Vice President George H. W. Bush faced image issues during his campaign for the republican presidential nomination. Fighting the perception that he was an elitist, as well as fallout from the Iran-Contra scandal and other Reagan administration initiatives, Bush's team

Vice President George H. W. Bush is pictured at a press conference in Nashua, New Hampshire, during the 1988 presidential campaign. *(George Bush Presidential Library)*

tried to make him seem strong and forceful. Bush played along, famously barking at anchorman Dan Rather in an interview following a report that emphasized the Iran-Contra scandal.

The vice president faced early competition from Senator Bob Dole, Congressman Jack Kemp, and televangelist Pat Robertson. Robertson fared well in the Michigan primary, and Dole walked away with victory in the Iowa caucuses, in which Bush came in third. A Bush victory in the New Hampshire primary was largely the result of Governor John Sununu's support and was key to Bush's success.

In the Democratic camp, various contenders threw their hats in the ring, although Senator Edward Kennedy of Massachusetts and Governor Mario Cuomo of New York, two of the party's strongest leaders, did not enter the race. Colorado senator Gary Hart, Massachusetts governor Michael Dukakis, and civil rights leader the Reverend Jesse Jackson each vied for the nomination. Hart was sidetracked by stories in the press in May 1987 that he was a womanizer. Photos of the senator taken in Florida with a young woman named Donna Rice while his wife remained in Colorado led the senator to withdraw his candidacy. He reentered

The House and the Senate passed a bill in 1988 that provided compensation to the survivors of Japanese families who had been sent to internment camps during World War II.

President Reagan signed a bill providing up to $20,000 compensation to approximately 60,000 surviving members of Japanese families who had lived in internment camps during World War II. *(Ronald Reagan Presidential Library)*

the race early in 1988, but the scandal had done irreparable damage. Jackson did well in many primaries, garnering the total majority of the popular vote. However, his anti-Semitic (anti-Jewish) 1984 reference to New York City as "Hymie town" haunted him, and he lost the key New York State primary.

After the dust settled, Dukakis proved to be the strongest Democratic contender. The son of Greek immigrants who personified the American dream—his father graduated from Harvard Medical School and his mother from prestigius Bates College in Maine—Dukakis served four terms in the state legislature prior to being elected governor of Massachusetts in 1974. He lost the Democratic primary for governor in 1978, but regained it in 1982, and was reelected in 1986. Dukakis was credited with helping Massachusetts bounce back from the recession of the early 1980s. Ultimately, Dukakis won the Democratic nomination and faced Bush.

The Bush campaign attacked Dukakis's policies as governor, including what they considered to be his soft stance on crime. In particular, the Republican Party focused on an incident involving Willie Horton, a convicted murderer and rapist who was given permission to leave prison for 10 weekends due to a special Massachusetts program. In 1987 while on leave, Horton attacked a couple in their Maryland home, stabbing the man and raping the woman. Although the Bush campaign did not specifically name Horton in an ad, they did create a commercial showing inmates walking through prison turnstiles with copy that lambasted Dukakis's record on crime. Ironically, the inmates in the commercials were young Republicans from Brigham Young University wearing borrowed state prison uniforms. In addition, for a short time the National Security Political Action Committee ran advertisements that actually showed Horton's image. Bush also alluded to Horton and the 1987 incident in many speeches during the campaign.

Former Reagan speechwriter Peggy Noonan scripted Bush's acceptance speech for the Republican National Convention. He responded to accusations that he would raise taxes with the most famous line of his campaign: "Read my lips. No new taxes." While accepting the GOP nomination, Bush spoke of a "kinder, gentler nation" that embraced volunteerism and called volunteers "a thousand points of light." Bush's strong presence and sound bite-worthy speech overshadowed the concerns that many had about his choice of a running mate, Senator Dan Quayle of Indiana. First as a congressman and later as a senator, Quayle had an abysmal attendance record. Most important, however, Quayle did not appear particularly mature or intelligent. When Bush announced Quayle as his running mate, the junior senator playfully jabbed at the vice president and said, "Go get 'em!"

Despite Dukakis's best attempts to portray himself as a strong and competent candidate, he lost the momentum he had gained immediately following the Democratic Convention. Footage of Dukakis wearing a too-large military helmet while riding in an M-1 tank during a visit to a General Dynamics plant quickly became a punch line. The Bush team, in fact, acquired the image and used it in a pro-Bush advertisement. A poor showing at the second presidential debate, in which Dukakis appeared cold and aloof, seemed to seal his fate. When asked if he would throw his support behind the death penalty if his wife Kitty were raped and murdered, he showed no emotion, a reaction that did not win him any supporters. In the end, George H. W. Bush was elected in November.

George H. W. Bush became the first vice president to take office following a two-term president since Martin Van Buren succeeded Andrew Jackson in 1836. Bush received 53.4 percent of the popular vote (48,886,097), and 426 Electoral College votes in the November 8 election, while Dukakis received 45.6 per-

COMMON GROUND

Jesse Jackson's speech before the 1988 Democratic National Convention was one of his most inspiring.

Common ground: America is not a blanket woven from one thread, one color, one cloth. When I was a child growing up in Greenville, South Carolina, my grandmamma could not afford a blanket, she didn't complain and we did not freeze. Instead she took pieces of old cloth—patches, wool, silk, gabardine, crockersack—only patches, barely good enough to wipe off your shoes with. But they didn't stay that way very long. With sturdy hands and a strong cord, she sewed them together into a quilt, a thing of beauty and power and culture.... Be as wise as my grandmamma. Pull the patches and the pieces together, bound by a common thread. When we form a great quilt of unity and common ground, we'll have the power to bring about health care and housing and jobs and education and hope to our nation.

cent of the popular vote (41,809,074) and 111 Electoral College votes. Libertarian candidate Ron Paul received .5 percent of the popular vote (432,179). Voter turnout was the lowest since 1942. Bush's victory, however, was not as definitive as his predecessor's was in 1980. Reagan had received 500,000 more votes overall and had won states that Bush failed to carry.

Despite losing the presidency, Democrats gained one seat in the Senate and two seats in the House, giving them control of both houses. This had not occurred since 1960. As president, Bush would have to contend with 55 Democrats and 45 Republicans in the Senate, and 262 Democrats and 173 Republicans in the House.

FOREIGN AFFAIRS

In March 1988, the Iran-Iraq war intensified. Iraq increased missile attacks and the use of chemical weapons on Iranian cities. The Kurdish population of Iraq was also subjected to chemical weapons, and thousands of civilians were killed. Minor skirmishes between the United States military and Iran increased during the spring of 1988. On July 30, 1988, 290 passengers aboard an Iranian jet perished when the

An Iranian jet was accidentally shot down by the USS *Vincennes,* an American warship stationed in the Persian Gulf, on July 30, 1988, resulting in the deaths of 290 passengers. *(DOD Defense Visual Information Center)*

TRAGEDY OVER SCOTLAND

On December 21, 1988, Pan Am flight 103 blew up over Lockerbie, Scotland. All 259 passengers and crew aboard were killed, along with 11 people on the ground in Lockerbie. It was later determined that Libyan terrorists were to blame for placing the bomb on the plane, which was inside a radio-cassette player.

An aerial photo shows destruction in Lockerbie, Scotland, from the crash of Pan Am 103. (AP/Wide World Photos)

plane was accidentally shot down by the USS *Vincennes,* an American warship in the Persian Gulf.

Reagan and Gorbachev met in Moscow in May 1988, their fourth summit in two and one-half years. During their meeting in Moscow, Reagan and Gorbachev agreed to an exchange program of 1,000 students each year, and to provide each other advance notice of any missile testing.

In December 1988, Gorbachev made a speech to the United Nations in which he announced that he would reduce the Soviet military by 20 percent, or 500,000 people. In addition, he planned to cut the Soviet military presence in eastern Europe. He seemed to be steering the superpower in a new, less aggressive direction.

The all-star benefit concerts continued as artists like Bruce Springsteen, Tracy Chapman, Peter Gabriel, and Sting hit the road on a tour benefiting the human rights organization Amnesty International.

On February 21, 1988, prominent televangelist Jimmy Swaggart announced during a taping of his television show that he was temporarily stepping down from the pulpit because he was guilty of a sin that he would not specify. Swaggart later admitted to having relations with prostitutes and gave up his television ministry.

TELEVISION AND MUSIC

Throughout 1988, NBC dominated the prime time ratings, finishing first for the fourth year in a row. Sitcoms such as *The Cosby Show, A Different World, Cheers, Golden Girls,* and *Night Court* kept the network at the top. Still, network primetime viewing declined by 8 percent overall for the big three networks as they competed with cable and video. A strike by the Writer's Guild of America began in March and lasted through August, delaying the start of the season until late October.

Rapper LL Cool J represented the romantic side of rap, scoring big with his first Top 40 hit, "I Need Love" in 1988 and the Top 40 crossover hit "I'm Going Back to Cali." Female rappers Salt-N-Pepa scored their first gold single with "Push It." Bobby Brown broke away from the boy group New Edition and hit the charts with "Don't Be Cruel" and "My Prerogative."

Former GoGo's lead singer Belinda Carlisle also found success as a solo artist with "I Get Weak" and "Heaven Is a Place on Earth." Australian band INXS enjoyed the success of multiple singles from their album *Kick.* Guns N' Roses had their first hit with "Sweet Child O' Mine" from *Appetite for Destruction.* Whitney Houston made history by becoming the first artist to have an album spawn four singles that hit number one on the Billboard chart. Michael Jackson

Compact disc (CD) sales surpassed the sales of vinyl albums for the first time in 1988. *(Michele L. Camardella)*

JESUS AT THE MOVIES

Acclaimed director Martin Scorsese, whose previous celebrated films included *Taxi Driver, Raging Bull, The Last Waltz,* and *The King of Comedy,* stirred up controversy with *The Last Temptation of Christ* in 1988. Based on the 1955 novel by Nikos Kazantzakis, the film painted Christ in a more human light, and included scenes in which he imagined marriage and intimate relations with Mary Magdalene. Many religious leaders refused to attend a preview screening arranged by Scorsese. Protests and boycotts were organized by conservative Christians, many of whom had either never viewed the film or had seen a bootleg version that included scenes that did not make the final cut.

broke this record one month later, when his album *Bad* produced five number one songs.

April 2, 1988, marked the first time that all of the albums on the Billboard Hot 200 Albums chart were also available on CD. The sale of CDs also surpassed the sale of vinyl LPs for the first time in 1988, with CD sales increasing 31 percent from the previous year and LP sales decreasing 33 percent.

FILM

Movies about the Vietnam War continued in 1988 with *Distant Thunders* and *Off Limits.* Tom Cruise played a slick con artist with an autistic brother, played by Dustin Hoffman—who received the Oscar for his performance—in *Rain Man.* Harrison Ford starred as a businessman who falls for a secretary posing as an executive (Melanie Griffith) in the romantic comedy *Working Girl,* while *Crossing Delancey* featured Amy Irving as a New York City intellectual who is wooed by Sam (Peter Reigert), a Lower East Side pickle-maker.

Directed by Steven Spielberg, *Who Framed Roger Rabbit?* combined live actors with animated cartoon characters. Bruce Willis became an action hero in *Die Hard.* Former child star Jodie Foster emerged as a serious adult actress with *The Accused,* for which she won the Best Actress Oscar. Action movie star Arnold Schwarzenegger turned to comedy with *Twins,* also starring Danny DeVito of *Taxi* fame.

SPORTS

Katarina Witt of East Germany won the gold in figure skating at the Winter Olympics in Calgary, Alberta, Canada, while American Brian Boitano took the gold in the men's competition. American Bonnie Blair walked away with the gold in the 500m speed-skating competition. In the 1988 Summer Olympics in Seoul,

Michael Jackson's popularity rose to new heights with the release of *Bad,* which had five number one hits. *(Paul Natkin/Photo Reserve)*

Video game fans were addicted to Tetris, which was designed in the USSR.

Canadian athlete Ben Johnson was stripped of his Olympic gold medal for the 100-meter track-and-field event after he tested positive for steroid use. *(AP/Wide World Photos)*

South Korea, Greg Louganis won the gold medal in springboard diving despite receiving five stitches after hitting his head on the diving board a week earlier. Sisters-in-law Jackie Joyner-Kersee and Florence Griffith Joyner each set world records during the Olympics, where they won a combined total of six medals—five gold and one silver.

The headlines were captured by Canadian sprinter Ben Johnson, who tested positive for drug use and was stripped of his gold medal for the 100m. Johnson also set a new world record during that race. Olympic officials sent Johnson home when test results indicated steroid use although the athlete blamed the results on an herbal tea he drank prior to the race.

The Edmonton Oilers won their fourth Stanley Cup in five years in May. Martina Navratilova lost the women's singles tennis championship at Wimbledon to Steffi Graf, ending her record-setting six-year winning streak. The Los Angeles Dodgers defeated the Oakland Athletics to clinch the World Series.

SCIENCE AND TECHNOLOGY

Both Retin-A and Rogaine surfaced in the war against aging in 1988. The topical acne medication Retin-A was touted as an anti-wrinkle treatment. Rogaine, meanwhile, offered hope for those with certain types of hair loss.

A flight by the space shuttle *Discovery* in October 1988 was the first shuttle mission launched following the *Challenger* explosion. *(National Aeronautics and Space Administration, NASA)*

The space shuttle *Discovery* completed a five-day mission in October 1988, marking the first shuttle flight since the *Challenger* accident. A whopping $2.4 billion dollars in design changes were made to the shuttle prior to the mission. In medicine, the first heart-lung transfer was completed in Baltimore, Maryland, on May 11. The United States took formal steps to reduce acid rain when it signed a United Nations protocol calling for emission rates to remain at 1987 levels.

A genetically engineered mouse was patented by Harvard University. The mouse was susceptible to cancer and intended for use in medical experiments. This led to much debate in terms of legal, political, and moral issues related to the impact of genetically altered animals on the economy, biosphere, and research.

THE FIGHT AGAINST AIDS

In May 1988, the United States launched its first coordinated public education campaign about AIDS, distributing 107 million copies of a booklet entitled "Understanding AIDS" attributed to Surgeon General C. Everett Koop. On October 11, ACT

A scientist tests water for evidence of acid rain. *(NOAA)*

After surveying some 15,000 veterans, the U.S. Center for Disease Control's Vietnam Experience Study found that Vietnam veterans who saw combat suffered more commonly from serious psychological problems 15 to 20 years after the war (which began in 1954 and ended in 1975) than veterans of that period who did not see combat.

FASHION FORWARD

With sales in women's fashion lagging throughout the late 1980s, it became clear that women were increasingly unhappy with their options. High-end fashion designer Donna Karan joined other designers who had launched lower-priced lines with Donna Karan New York (DKNY), offering quality pieces at half the price of her regular line. Still pricey at $100 to $700 per item, the line was geared toward working women.

At the same time, designer Norma Kamali added a dress line to her sportswear collections. Her patterned suits were worn with lots of jewelry and accessories.

Norma Kamali popularized the luxurious look of the late 1980s. *(Norma Kamali)*

UP shut down the Food and Drug Administration (FDA) headquarters when more than 1,000 protesters converged to demand a speedier drug approval process regarding AIDS-related drugs. In addition, experimental needle exchange programs started in New York City and San Francisco in an attempt to avoid transmission between IV drug users using dirty needles. Because Congress would not fund needle exchange programs, no federal funding was used.

CHAPTER 7

A NEW PRESIDENT AND THE 1980s LEGACY, 1989

President Reagan walks through the White House on his last day in office. *(Ronald Reagan Library)*

O N JANUARY 11, 1989, PRESIDENT Ronald Reagan made his last televised address from the White House Oval Office. In his final speech, he concluded with the following:

We've done our part. And as I walk off into the city streets, a final word to the men and women of the Reagan revolution, the men and women across America who for eight years did the work that brought America back. My friends: We did it. We weren't just marking time. We made a difference. We made the city stronger, we made the city freer, and we left her in good hands. All in all, not bad, not bad at all.

Ronald Reagan left the presidency with the highest popularity of any president since the polls were introduced in the 1930s.

THE REAGAN REVOLUTION RECAPPED

Reagan's years as president were in many ways a roller coaster ride. Unemployment rates, interest rates, and funding for social programs dropped while the federal deficit, defense spending, and the national debt soared. The number of homeless swelled, partly due to the cuts made in social service programs. The rich benefited from tax cuts and made more money while the poor made less money. Women and children were the most likely to be poverty-stricken.

Reagan, simultaneously known as the Great Communicator and the Teflon President, due to the way that criticism just rolled off of him, was decidedly hands off regarding many matters. He was even known to doze off during meetings, and, at times, he seemed blissfully oblivious to the severity of situations. On a trip to West Germany, he visited a cemetery in Bitburg, where 47 members of the Adolf Hitler's guard were buried, despite requests from humanitarian and Jewish groups to decline the invitation. In response to public outcry, a visit to the concentration camp at Bergen-Belsen that Reagan had originally declined was added to the itinerary.

At the end of Reagan's tenure, the economy appeared to have improved—at least on the surface. At 5.3 percent, unemployment was the lowest since 1974, and inflation was relatively stable at 4.4 percent. In addition, over the course of Reagan's presidency, 15 million new jobs became available. All in all, the rich got richer during the Reagan years, as the wealthiest 1 percent of

Americans possessed 15 percent of the national income, an increase from 8.1 percent at the beginning of the decade. Similarly, those in the top 20 percent of America's wealthiest households enjoyed a 14 percent increase in income. Meanwhile, the average income of the population's poorest decreased by $1,300 annually.

Upon leaving the White House, President and Mrs. Reagan retired to Bel-Air, California. He wrote his memoirs and collected large sums for public speaking engagements. In 1994, Reagan announced that he was suffering from Alzheimer's disease. On June 5, 2004, Ronald Reagan died at the age of 93.

THE NEW REGIME

George H. W. Bush was sworn in as the 42nd president on Friday, January 20, 1989, nearly 200 years after George Washington's inauguration. Many perceived his inaugural address as critical of the Reagan era. Bush discussed the need for bipartisanship, mentioned the importance of helping the homeless, noted that the deficit had to be brought down, and admonished that money and possessions are not the most important things in life, a direct criticism, it would seem, of the materialistic yuppie lifestyle. He repeatedly intoned that a "new breeze" was blowing, seemingly indicating that a change in policy was necessary.

Early on, Bush made it clear that he was not Reagan and that his administration would make its own decisions. Staffers remaining from the previous administration were notified they should be out of their offices by January 20, 1989. Still, Bush did maintain seven cabinet members that had served in the Reagan administration. James Baker moved from secretary of the Treasury to secretary of state, Lauren Cavasos remained secretary of education, and Richard Thornburgh stayed on as attorney general. Clayton Yuetter shifted to the Department of Agriculture from the role of U.S. trade representative,

George Bush was sworn in as the 42nd president of the United States of America on January 20, 1989. *(George Bush Presidential Library)*

"...I see history as a book with many pages, and each day we fill a page with acts of hopefulness and meaning."

—George H. W. Bush, inaugural address, January 20, 1989

and Elizabeth Dole shifted gears from the Department of Transportation to secretary of labor. Additional appointees included those to whom Bush owed political debts, including John Tower, who Bush named as secretary of defense on December 16, 1988.

Tower had a reputation in Washington, D.C., as a heavy drinker and womanizer, and there were questions about his consulting work for defense contractors and his alleged misappropriation of leftover campaign funds. Despite Tower's best efforts to prove that he would be a reliable defense secretary, Congress voted against his confirmation by a vote of 53 to 47 on March 9, 1989, the first such action since 1959. Bush replaced Tower with House minority whip Richard Cheney, a Republican from Wyoming who was sworn in on March 17, 1989, the same day that the Senate voted 92-0 in his favor. Republican Newt Gingrich from Georgia assumed Cheney's vacated position as House minority whip.

A KINDER, GENTLER NATION

Despite Bush's promises of a kinder, gentler nation, he vetoed a bill that Congress had passed that would raise the minimum wage from $3.35 per to $4.55 per hour. Congress failed to override the June 13 veto. A compromise was signed into law by President Bush in November 1989 and raised the minimum wage from $3.35 to $4.25 over the course of two years.

In 1989, Democratic senator Wendell H. Ford from Kentucky introduced a bill that would make voter registration easier by providing registration materials at public offices, such as the department of motor vehicles, public assistance offices, and military recruitment offices. Patrons of these offices would automatically be registered to vote upon the completion of voter registration forms available there. The Republicans successfully blocked the passage of the bill.

On June 21, 1989, the Supreme Court ruled that burning the American flag was protected by the First Amendment and was a form of freedom of speech. As a result, all state laws regarding the desecration of the flag were deemed invalid. Bush reacted by seeking a Constitutional amendment that would protect the flag. In response, Speaker of the House Thomas Foley offered the Flag Protection Act of 1989, which was passed by the Senate on October 15. The new law was ruled unconstitutional by a federal judge the following February, and when appealed to the Supreme Court, was again deemed unconstitutional in June 1990. A proposed amendment was defeated in both the House and the Senate in June of that year as well.

In a decision handed down on July 3, 1989, in the case of *Webster v. Reproductive Health Services of Missouri*, the Supreme Court ruled that states could impose restrictions on abortions. Much to the dismay of the religious right, however, the Court did not reverse *Roe v. Wade*, the landmark 1973 decision that deemed the regulation of abortion by states unconstitutional. In response, Bush declared his support for an amendment banning abortion. Congress, however, had other ideas, and submitted legislation designed to loosen the federal restrictions on abortion, all of which was vetoed by the president. Almost one quarter of the 43 bills that Bush vetoed during his presidency were abortion-related.

In March 1989, Congress slashed the budget of the National Endowment for the Arts (NEA) by $45,000 in response to the group's support of controversial art exhibits. In particular, the homoerotic work of the late Robert Mapplethorpe, a photographer, came under fire. In a charge led by conservative North Carolina senator Jesse Helms, Congress also passed a bill that banned federal funding of overtly sexual, sado-masochistic, or homoerotic art.

The new president also continued to wage a war on drugs. In his first televised address on September 5,

President George H. W. Bush is pictured with Vice President Dan Quayle. *(George Bush Presidential Library)*

The number of skinheads — traditionally associated with neo-Nazi groups in the United States—grew from less than 100 in 1980 to more than 5,000 by the end of the decade.

President Bush, seen here at The President's Education Summit for Governors, made education a major point in his campaign platform. *(George Bush Presidential Library)*

THE FEMINIZATION OF POVERTY

By the end of the decade, unwed mothers accounted for 25 percent of all births. The cycle of poverty often continued for these women, many of whom were African American or Hispanic. They were less likely to finish high school, attend college, or have a job that paid enough to keep them above the poverty level. In addition, throughout the 1980s, the Reagan administration cut programs such as Women-Infants-Children (WIC), which aided in the reduction of infant mortality rates by providing both prenatal and post-natal care.

1989, Bush announced a $7.9 billion plan in which almost half would go toward law enforcement initiatives. Congress ultimately passed an $8.8 billion bill in 1990, adding $900 million for treatment and education programs to Bush's initial proposal.

During the 1988 campaign, Bush had positioned himself as the education president, recommending primarily that better use be made of existing funds with modest additional funding. He also advocated rewarding schools that showed marked improvement with underprivileged children and providing pay incentives for outstanding teachers. In fall 1989, the president held a summit on education for American governors, during which it was agreed that national performance standards would be established.

On Friday, October 13, 1989, the stock market fell 190 points, marking its biggest drop since the so-called Black Monday of 1987. As 1989 drew to a close a recession seemed inevitable. Inflation had risen to 5 percent in 1989, increasing steadily from 1.9 percent in 1986 to 3.7 percent in 1987, then 4.8 percent in 1988.

IRAN-CONTRAL SCANDAL

Oliver North was tried on 12 felony counts in May 1989. He contended that his superiors had ordered him to remain silent about the arms for hostages operation. On May 3, 1989, he was convicted on three counts—accepting an illegal gratuity, obstructing Congress, and destroying documents. He received a light sentence that included 1,200 hours of community service, two years probation, and a $150,000 fine. Upon his appeal in 1990, one conviction was overturned and the other two were set aside on the basis that North's televised testimony may have influenced trial witnesses.

THE INVASION OF PANAMA

Panamanian leader General Manuel Noriega lost the presidential election held on May 7, 1989. The shady leader had received $322,000 over the years in cash and gifts as a CIA informant and a link to provide arms to the Nicaraguan Contra rebels. Noriega declared the elections null. In addition, Guillermo Endara, who had won the vice-presidential election, was beaten bloody by Noriega's personal police force, the Dignity Battalions. Ousting Noriega became a huge priority for Bush, whose national security team began to consider various options. On December 16, 1989, two separate attacks on U.S. soldiers who were on leave in Panama ultimately prompted military action.

At 1:00 A.M. on December 20, 1989, 12,000 U.S. troops invaded Panama with the objective of deposing General Manuel Noriega. They joined the 10,500 troops that were already stationed in the country. Guillermo Endara had been sworn in as the new president of Panama barely 20 minutes earlier. The U.S. soldiers took control of Panama City and the area surrounding the city within 72 hours, but they failed to capture Noriega. On Christmas Eve, Noriega gained temporary sanctuary at the Vatican Embassy but surrendered on January 3, 1990, after U.S. troops directed loud rock and roll music at the building. The invasion led to the death of 23 U.S. soldiers and allegedly thousands of Panamanians. Noriega was extradited to the United States, where he stood trial and was sentenced to jail time.

In December 1989, 12,000 U.S. troops invaded Panama in an effort to depose General Manuel Noriega. *(DOD Defense Visual Information Center.)*

THE USSR

During Reagan's second term, the United States and Soviet Union had moved steadily toward disarmament. Bush wanted to take things more slowly and initiated what the Soviets called the "pauza," or pause, during which his administration considered how to proceed. Bush and Gorbachev did not resume discussions until December 1988 at the Malta Summit, which took place aboard the cruise ship *Maxim Gorky*. Gorbachev continued to reduce the Soviet military presence in 1989. The last Soviet troops were withdrawn from Afghanistan, and submarine patrols in the Caribbean and near the U.S. coast also ceased.

By January 1989, Poland's Solidarity movement was robust (Solidarity was a union movement opposed to Soviet-controlled communism in Poland.). In a surprise move, the Communist Party decided to allow free elections for the upper house of the Polish parliament. In return, the Communist Party, along with its allies, would retain control of the lower house. In the June 1989 elections, 99 of the 100 seats in the upper house went to Solidarity. Although candidates in the lower house ran unopposed, 33 of the 35 top Communist leaders lost their seats because their names were crossed out on the ballots by more than half of the voters.

Soviet General Secretary Gorbachev and President Bush are pictured on the cruise ship *Maxim Gorky* at the Malta Summit. *(George Bush Presidential Library)*

In August, as the Solidarity and Communist leaders were in the midst of negotiating a coalition government, Gorbachev and Polish general secretary Mieczyslaw Rakowski spent 40 minutes on the telephone allegedly discussing the democratization of Poland. In a historic election a few days later, Solidarity adviser Tadeusz Mazowiecki won the prime minister's seat.

As Poland underwent historic change, other eastern European countries followed suit. Hungary had removed a border fence with Austria, allowing East Germans to move into West Germany, thus breaking a 1968 treaty with East Germany. Over the course of three days in September 1989, more than 13,000 East Germans fled eastern Europe via Hungary. One month later, the Hungarian Socialist Workers became the first ruling Communist Party to officially abandon the Communist ideology.

An October 1989 visit to East Germany by Gorbachev sparked protests against the Communist Party and in favor of Gorbachev's new, lenient attitude. On November 4, more than 500,000 protesters demonstrated in East Berlin, while an additional 500,000 protested in other cities. As a result, Prime Minister Willi Stoph and his cabinet resigned. Exactly five days later, on November 9, points where people could pass through were opened in the Berlin Wall. Soon after, jubilant Berliners were chipping away at

On November 7, 1989, David Dinkins was elected the first African-American mayor of New York City.

EDGING TOWARD DEMOCRACY

In spring 1989, student protesters numbering in the hundreds of thousands began to demand democracy in China. Congregated in Tiananmen Square in Beijing, the protesters, now numbering nearly 1 million and including people from all walks of life, seemed to be near a nonviolent resolution and the end of the communism. However, on June 5, 1989, the Chinese military faced off against the students, wounding more than 10,000 protesters and killing 3,000 in the process. The most provocative image for many was a lone young man standing unarmed in defiance before a line of military tanks, moving first right then left to block their advance, finally jumping on top of the tank's gun, and ultimately descending back into a waiting crowd. The Bush administration offered sharp criticism of the Chinese government's actions, delaying a loan extension and suspending arm sales to the country.

Employees and former employees from MTM Enterprises, the production company responsible for *The Mary Tyler Moore Show*, were involved with more than a dozen popular shows throughout the 1980s, including: *Hill Street Blues, St. Elsewhere, thirtysomething, Moonlighting, The Cosby Show, Family Ties, Miami Vice, Twin Peaks,* and *Taxi.*

"Don't have a cow, dude!"

—Bart Simpson, *The Simpsons*

the barrier, bringing the wall down after almost three decades of division.

Soon, the Velvet Revolution swept Czechoslovakia as well. Demonstrations were held in response to reports of police brutality against a student at a rally in Prague. Increasingly large numbers of protesters gathered, beginning with 10,000 people on November 19, and culminating with 350,000 on November 23 and 24. General Secretary Milos Jakes and his 12-member cabinet resigned, and a general strike froze the capital and the country as protests continued to attract more supporters. Ultimately, in early December, President Gustav Husak, a former Communist Party leader, resigned, and was succeeded by playwright and opposition spokesperson Vaclav Havel.

TELEVISION

The popularity of cable television grew throughout the 1980s. By the end of the decade, 60 percent of all households received basic cable. Over two dozen cable networks existed, many devoted to a particular subject such as music, sports, or news. Arsenio Hall made history as the first black, male nightly talk show host. *Seinfeld* premiered, and viewers became addicted to a show about, well, nothing. The animated series *The Simpsons* also aired for the first time.

FILM, MUSIC, AND BOOKS

Cameron Crowe wrote and directed *Say Anything*, featuring John Cusack as an all-around nice guy underachiever who falls in love with his class valedictorian. This unlikely love story was a more mature, realistic depiction of teenage romance than many of the preceding Brat Pack films. The black comedy *Heathers*, meanwhile, took a look at the darker side of high school life and teenage popularity.

Batman, directed by Tim Burton, brought the comic book hero to life and offered numerous merchandising opportunities. Adventure hero Indiana Jones teamed up with his father, played by Sean Connery, for *Indiana Jones and the Last Crusade.* Jessica Tandy received the Oscar for Best Actress for the charming *Driving Miss Daisy,* also starring Morgan Freeman. Director Steven Soderbergh made his feature film debut with *Sex, Lies and Videotape,* and Billy Crystal and Meg Ryan debated whether or not men and women can be just friends in *When Harry Met Sally. Casualties of War, Born on the Fourth of July,* and *In Country*—all movies related to the Vietnam War—were also released in 1989.

MTV was instrumental in making rap even more popular with mainstream audiences. The music channel began airing the specialty show *Yo! MTV Raps* in 1989, which soon became their most popular show. Rap also continued to grow as a creative art form. In response to the rap that was produced on the East Coast, the subgenre gangsta rap emerged from the West Coast. Gangsta rap represented urban life on the streets, including gangs, violence, and a threatening police force. N.W.A. best personified gangsta rap with their release *Straight Outta Compton* (1989).

Former teen idol Donny Osmond made a comeback with "Soldier of Love." The boy band New Kids on the Block had teenage girls everywhere "Hangin' Tough." In an embarrassing turn of events, British pop duo Milli Vanilli received the 1989 Grammy Award for Best New Artist. They would return it when rumors that they did not actually sing on their hit record proved to be true.

The sale of books doubled over the course of the 1980s, hitting almost $15 billion by the end of the decade. Top selling authors included master of horror Stephen King and queen of the romance saga Danielle Steele. In 1989, Salman Rushdie's *The Satanic Verses* caused Ayatollah Khomeini to issue a death threat against all involved with its publication, sending Rushdie into hiding.

"...police think they have the authority to kill a minority!"

—N.W.A, "F—— tha Police," *Straight Outta Compton,* 1989

Public Enemy, featuring Flavor Flav (pictured) used rap to give a voice to the disenfranchised. *(Paul Natkin/Photo Reserve)*

EARTHQUAKE!

San Francisco was rocked by an earthquake of immense magnitude on October 17, 1989. Registering 6.9 on the Richter scale, the quake damaged 100,000 buildings. The catastrophe left 63 people dead and more than 3,700 injured. The injury and death tolls would likely have been much higher except that many people held gone home early to watch the third game of the World Series, which was being played that day at Candlestick Park.

The Lomo Prieta earthquake damaged 100,000 buildings and interrupted the World Series. *(San Francisco History Center)*

SPORTS

By the end of the 1980s, there were more than 20,000 health clubs in the United States, a huge increase from the 7,500 that existed at the beginning of the decade. In October 1989, hockey superstar Wayne Gretsky became the leading scorer in National Hockey League (NHL) history when he scored his 1,850th point. In his 303rd game Michael Jordan of the Chicago Bulls, scored his 10,000th National Basketball Association point.

In August 1989, baseball legend Pete Rose—who in 1985 had his 4,192nd career hit, breaking Ty Cobb's 1928 record—was banned from Major League baseball. Upon his retirement in 1988, Rose held 34 major league and National League records. In 1989, as manager of the Cincinnati Reds, Rose was accused of betting on baseball, and banned from the game for life, although he retained the right to request reinstatement. In other baseball news, as president of the National League, Bill White became the first African American to be appointed the head of a major professional sports league in the United States. Billy Martin, meanwhile, former New York Yankee player and manager, was killed in a drunk driving accident.

SCIENCE AND TECHNOLOGY

The personal computer industry topped $70 billion as the 1980s neared an end. PCs continued to be a fixture not only in offices and businesses, but also in homes. During the 1990s, the PC would become even more indispensable with the advent of the Internet. The Sega Genesis was released on January 9, giving video game fans a new reason to rejoice. The handheld Nintendo device *Game Boy* was released in 1989, allowing video game aficionados to take their games with them wherever they went.

The U.S. National Institute of Health launched the Human Genome Project, meant to map the human genome, or the 3 billion nucleotides that compose the genetic sequence. This multibillion dollar project was

ENVIRONMENTAL CRISIS: *EXXON VALDEZ*

On March 24, 1989, Alaska suffered the largest oil spill in North American history when the oil tanker *Exxon Valdez* struck the Bligh Reef in Prince William Sound. Captain Joseph J. Hazlewood had turned control of the *Valdez* over to his third mate Gregory Cousins and helmsman Robert Kagen, neither of whom were licensed to pilot the ship. Almost 900 square feet of shoreline were covered by the approximately 10.9 million gallons of oil that spilled. The affected areas included five state parks, three national parks, a national forest, four national wildlife refuges, a state game sanctuary, and four areas deemed as critical habitats. In addition, more than 23 species were killed or injured by the spill, including bald eagles, river otters, killer whales, mussels, and harbor seals. The cleanup cost Exxon more than $2 billion, and ultimately included help from U.S. troops. Exxon paid an additional $1 billion fine, much of which was paid to local fisherman whose business had been disrupted by the spill. As a result of the spill, new legislation was introduced that required newly built oil tankers to have double hulls.

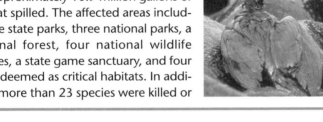

Environmentalists tried to save wildlife such as this bird from the effects of the oil spill. *(NOAA)*

funded by tax dollars, and it ultimately intended to offer insight into the brain and human intelligence, as well as genetic diseases.

By mid-1989, there were 1,224 toxic dump sites on the Superfund cleanup list. The Superfund had $8.5 billion earmarked for toxic site cleanup. In the fight against ozone-depletion and CFCs, countries in the European Economic Communities (EEC) agreed to stop CFC production by the year 2000. Later in 1989 in Helsinki, 81 countries would agree to do the same, including the United States.

AIDS cases continued to increase at an alarming rate. There were 142,000 reported cases by 1989, but it was widely assumed that there might have been as many as an additional 260,000 unreported cases. Strides continued to be made in the use of AZT to treat AIDS. Trials showed that the drug slowed the advent of the disease in HIV-positive patients.

THE END OF AN ERA
The 1980s were defined by Ronald Reagan's presidency. His charisma and formidable presence translated

More than 1,200 toxic dump sites were included on the Superfund list by mid-1989. Many sites held hundreds of 55-gallon drums, such as those shown here full of unidentified chemicals. *(U.S. Fish and Wildlife Service)*

incredibly well in his television addresses and public appearances. Reagan instilled a sense of patriotism in many Americans that had dwindled throughout the 1970s. Reagan clearly stood for democracy and against communism, as well as for a new focus on morality. The release of the American hostages being held in Iran—negotiated by the Carter administration—on the day of Reagan's inauguration seemed to usher in a new era, one in which America again stood proud and strong.

Still, despite Reagan's public popularity, his tenure was not without controversy. The economy was unstable, social programs were cut or had their budgets reduced, and the federal deficit surged. The poor remained poor and actually experienced a decrease in income, while the wealthiest in the nation became richer and benefited from tax cuts. The invasion of Grenada proved an unpopular move with the rest of the world. The disclosure that the United States had, in fact, traded arms for hostages after the president's clear denial of such action also was cause for concern.

The focus on morality and a return to traditional values resulted in a new film rating, PG-13, noting materials eligible for children 13 and under, as well as requests from the PMRC to institute warning labels on records containing explicit lyrics. The abortion fight was also carried out under the banner of morality, even as abortion providers and clinic workers became subject of acts of violence condoned by the most radical pro-life groups. The question of morality also continued to be an issue for the Bush administration with Congress' slashing of the National Endowment for the Art's (NEA) budget in response to the group's commitment to support controversial art exhibits, as well as in the continued abortion fight and other areas. In addition, the ERA failed to garner enough support to be ratified, leaving women behind in their quest for equality.

Although Reagan, and subsequently Bush, supported traditional values, other cultural develop-

Ronald Reagan salutes from the presidential helicopter as he leaves the White House on his last day in office. *(Ronald Reagan Library)*

MTV VJ J. J. Jackson interviews Dave Stewart and Annie Lennox, the British pop duo known as the Eurythmics. MTV not only changed the way music was publicized and sold but also introduced middle America to new fashions, looks, hairstyles, and fads. *(MTV)*

ments remained more progressive. MTV changed the face of music and increased the emphasis on the artist's appearance. Rap music and heavy metal represented disenfranchised groups and gave them a voice. Films began to address homosexuality more openly in the early 1980s, and the advent of AIDS made everyone aware of homosexual issues. Television shows began to feature recurring gay characters.

As 1989 drew to a close, President Bush prepared to enter a new era. The 1990s promised to be bigger, better, and brighter than the 1980s. In particular, technological advancements promised faster, more efficient equipment that would ease work and home life. In short, the CD, fax machine, and personal computer were just the beginning. Bush also promised a country that was more attuned to the needs of its people, and a "kinder, gentler" nation. Thus, for many the 1990s began with a renewed optimism that the economy would remain healthy, and that Americans would enjoy peace and prosperity while others wondered if the 1990s would simply bring more of the same.

GLOSSARY

acid rain   Rain polluted by high levels of sulfuric and nitric acid from fossil fuel emissions.

Alzheimer's disease   A degenerative brain disease that results in memory loss.

acquired immune deficiency syndrome (AIDS)   Caused by the human immuno-deficiency virus (HIV), this disease attacks the immune system, leaving it vulnerable to numerous diseases.

Brat Pack   A group of teenage actors who starred in multiple coming-of-age films in the mid-1980s.

Carter Doctrine   President Carter's firm stance against the Soviet Union upon their invasion of Afghanistan.

compact disc (CD)   A thin round plastic piece on which digital data is stored.

Contras   Nicaraguan rebels who attempted to overthrow the country's Sandinista regime with assistance from the United States.

deregulation   The removal of previously enacted regulations or restrictions.

Equal Rights Amendment (ERA)   A constitutional amendment proposed in 1972 that called for equal rights for women. The ERA failed to be ratified.

facsimile (fax) machine   A machine that transfers text and images over telephone wires.

Food and Drug Administration (FDA)   Agency within the Department of Health and Human Services that tests and approves drugs, cosmetics, medical instruments, food, and biological products to ensure the public's health and safety.

glasnost   Soviet word meaning openness in communication and government decisions.

Iran-Contra scandal   A political scandal in which the United States sold illegal arms in an attempt to gain the freedom of American hostages and to illegally send money to Contras in Nicaragua.

Moral Majority   A political group founded by and devoted to forwarding the agenda of conservative Christian fundamentalists.

Music TeleVision (MTV)   Cable network that that delivers several channels of music videos and MTV network shows.

mutually assured destruction (MAD)   Theory that the world's superpowers keep each other in check by fearing each could destroy the other.

October surprise An event that occurs immediately prior to Election Day and affects the vote.

National Security Council (NSC) The primary internal body advising the president on national security, foreign policy, and domestic issues.

perestroika The political and economic reconstruction of the Soviet Union.

rap music An urban music genre that developed in the South Bronx, New York, that features rhyming lyrics and incorporates music, or sampling, from other songs.

Reaganomics An economic plan implemented by President Reagan that combined major tax cuts with cuts to social programs and increased military spending.

Reagan Doctrine A policy that sought to curb the growth and influence of communism, particularly in Latin America, through economic and military aid.

Sandinistas The Marxist-oriented government of Nicaragua.

savings and loans An alternative to banks offering both savings plans and a variety of loans.

skinhead Traditionally, in the United States, a white supremacist associated with the neo-Nazi movement.

stagflation The combination of high unemployment, high prices, and a stagnant economy.

Strategic Defense Initiative (SDI) Also known as Star Wars. A proposed anti-missile program that would protect the United States from both land and space.

Superfund Program Fund established to clean up and investigate abandoned hazardous waste sites.

supply-side economics The use of tax cuts to stimulate economic growth.

televangelist An evangelical preacher who uses television to communicate, hold services, and fund raise.

video cassette recorder (VCR) A recording machine that allows for the taping of television shows or the broadcast of prerecorded movies.

yuppie An acronym for young urban professional, defining an urban-dwelling, white-collar worker making more than $40,000 per year who engaged in status-conscious retail spending.

FURTHER READING

BOOKS

Abrams, Herbert L. *The President Has Been Shot.* New York and London: W.W. Norton & Company, 1992.

Altman, Dennis. *AIDS in the Mind of America.* Garden City, N.Y.: Doubleday, 1986.

Berman, Larry. *Looking Back on the Reagan Presidency.* Baltimore and London: Johns Hopkins University Press, 1990.

Blum, David. "The Brat Pack." *Chicago Tribune,* July 14, 1985, p. 16.

Blum, John M. *The National Experience.* San Diego: Harcourt Brace Jovanovich, 1989.

Brooks, Nancy Rivera. "1980s Shoppers Charged into a Brave New World of Goods." *The Los Angeles Times,* December 31, 1989, p. 1.

Buursma, Bruce. "The Week that Rocked Television Ministries." *Chicago Tribune,* March 29, 1987.

Campbell, Colin. *The Bush Presidency: First Appraisals.* Chatham, N.J.: Chatham House Publishers, 1991.

Campling, Elizabeth. *The 1980s: Portrait of a Decade.* London: B.T. Batsford, 1990.

Cannon, Lou. "Hard Shoes to Fill: Reagan Heads West with High Ratings, Leaving Vivid Memories and a Legacy of Many Successes, Notable Shortcomings." *The Washington Post,* January 20, 1980, p. f.10.

Carnegy, Vicky. *Fashions of a Decade: The 1980s.* New York: Facts On File, 1990.

Corey, Melinda and George Ochoa. *The American Film Institute Desk Reference.* London: Dorling Kindersley, 2002.

Cromartie, Michael, ed. *No Longer Exiles: The Religious New Right in American Politics.* Papers from Conference in Washington, D.C.: Ethics and Public Policy Center, 1990.

Daume, Daphne, and Louise Watson. *1987: Britannica Book of the Year.* Chicago: Encyclopedia Britannica, 1988.

———. *1988: Britannica Book of the Year.* Chicago: Encyclopedia Britannica, Inc., 1989.

Duignan, Peter, and Alvin Rabushka. *The United States in the 1980s.* Palo Alto, Calif.: Hoover Institution, Stanford University, 1980.

Evans, Rowland and Robert Novak, *The Reagan Revolution.* New York: E.P. Dutton, 1981.

Gergen, David R. "Unraveling of a Presidency." *U.S. News & World Report,* May 23, 1988.

Greene, Robert John. *The Presidency of George Bush.* Lawrence, Kans.: University Press of Kansas, 2000.

Hadden, Jeffrey K., and Anson Shupe. *Televangelism—Power and Politics on God's Frontier.* New York: Henry Holt, 1987.

Hargrove, Irwin C. *Jimmy Carter as President.* Baton Rouge: Louisiana State University Press, 1988.

Hill, Dilys M., and Phil Williams. *The Bush Presidency.* New York: St. Martin's Press, 1994.

Johnson, Haynes. *Sleepwalking Through History: America in the Reagan Years.* New York and London: W.W. Norton & Company, 1991.

Kallen, Stuart A. *The 1980s: A Cultural History of the United States Through the Decades.* San Diego: Lucent Books, Inc., 1999.

Kaufman, Burton I. *The Presidency of James Earl Carter, Jr.* Lawrence, Kans.: University Press of Kansas, 1993.

Levitan, Sar A., and Isaac Shapiro. *Working but Poor.* Baltimore: Johns Hopkins University Press, 1987.

Levy, Peter B. *Encyclopedia of the Reagan-Bush Years.* Westport, Conn.: Greenwood Press, 1996.

Lewis, Richard S. *Challenger: The Final Voyage.* New York: Columbia University Press, 1988.

Martin, William. *With God on Our Side.* New York: Broadway Books, 1996.

McCuen, Gary. *The Religious Right.* Madison, Wisc.: Gary E. McCuen Publications, 1989.

McGrath, Tom. *MTV: The Making of a Revolution.* Philadelphia and London: Running Press, 1996.

Payne, Anthony, Paul Sutton, and Tony Thorndike. *Grenada: Revolution and Invasion.* New York: St. Martin's Press, 1984.

Reagan, Ronald. *Ronald Reagan: An American Life.* New York: Simon and Schuster, 1990.

Schwartzberg, Renée. *Ronald Reagan.* World Leaders Past and Present. New York and Philadelphia: Chelsea House, 1991.

Seib, Gerald F. "Marines Complete Lebanon Withdrawal as Battleship's Guns Pound." *Wall Street Journal.* February 27, 1984, p. 1.

Sewall, Gilbert T. *The Eighties: A Reader.* Reading, Mass.: Addison-Wesley, 1997.

Solinger, Rickie. *Abortion Wars.* Berkeley, Calif.: University of California Press, 1998.

Sloan, John W. *The Reagan Effect: Economics and Professional Leadership.* Lawrence, Kans.: University Press of Kansas, 1999.

Solomon, Ezra. *Beyond the Turning Point.* San Francisco: W.H. Freeman, 1982.

Stark, Steven D. *Glued to the Set.* New York: The Free Press, 1997.

Thompson, Robert J. *Television's Second Golden Age.* New York: Continuum, 1996.

Torr, James D. *The 1980s.* San Diego: Greenhaven Press, 2000.

Walsh, Lawrence E. *Iran-Contra: The Final Report.* New York: Random House, 1994.

"The Living Legacy of Jim Bakker." *U.S. News & World Report*, November 6, 1989, p. 14.

WEBSITES

Avert.org. "The History of AIDS 1981–1986," Avert. URL: http://www.avert.org/his87_92.htm. Downloaded on January 18, 2004.

NASA. "The Crew of the Challenger Shuttle Mission in 1986," URL: http://www.hq.nasa.gov/office/pao/History/Biographies/challenger.html. Downloaded on May 2, 2004.

Ronald Reagan. "Iran-Contra Affair," CNN. URL: http://www.cnn.com/SPECIALS/2004/reagan/stories/speech.archive/iran.contra.html. "Just Say No," CNN. URL: http://www.cnn.com/SPECIALS/2004/reagan/stories/speech.archive/just.say.no.html. Downloaded on June 7, 2004.

United Nations Development Programme. "The Ozone Layer Problem." URL: http://www.undp.org/seed/eap/montreal/ozone.htm. Downloaded on October 17, 2004.

INDEX